A Guide for Men

THE
COURAGE
TO BE
HONEST

Facing Hidden Challenges
of the Heart

JOE STORR

To all men out there who want to grow.

©2024 by Joe Storr
Published by hope*books
2217 Matthews Township Pkwy
Suite D302
Matthews, NC 28105
www.hopebooks.com

hope*books is a division of hope*media
Printed in the United States of America by
hope*books

First paperback edition.
Paperback ISBN: 979-8-89185-036-1
Hardcover ISBN: 979-8-89185-037-8
Ebook ISBN: 979-8-89185-038-5
Library of Congress Number: 2023950995

hope*books

"He was a man all over, rounded and complete."
General William T. Sherman,
speaking of his friend, General Ulysses S. Grant

Acknowledgments

The most effective—and safest—way to help others is to never go it alone. I was fortunate to have sturdy support in preparation for this writing project and throughout its duration.

My father, Howard Storr, carefully reviewed every word I wrote, week by week. His perspective and feedback influenced not only the content but also my posture in writing it. Thanks, Dad. I've so enjoyed our partnership.

Bryan Johnson, my close friend, has been with me for much of my walk with Jesus and my ministry training. He has a pastor's heart, a theologian's mind, and exceptional discernment. Thanks, my friend, for your company and encouragement.

Karen Boden, this was your idea! Thanks for your friendship, for coaching me in the art and discipline of writing, and for spurring me on to put this book together.

Three of my seminary professors and colleagues, Dr. John Coe, Dr. Betsy Barber, and Dr. Judy TenElshof, gave me their love and guidance throughout my ministry training and beyond. Thank you, friends. You've been instrumental in my life.

Endorsements

"If you are interested in being the best 'you' that you can be, you owe it to yourself and your journey to read this new masterpiece from Joe Storr. Joe skillfully identifies how to navigate hidden obstacles and maps out practical steps to overcome them on our path to finding God's best for us."

—Clair Hoover, Executive Director,
National Coalition of Ministries to Men

"Deep inner change can be an uncomfortable and scary journey that requires great courage. You can trust Joe Storr to guide you. Joe is a gentle, compassionate, and wise guide who has been on his own deep journey of inner transformation and is passionate about helping other men. If you're looking for growth, healing, and greater wholeness in Christ, your time spent with Joe in this book could prove very rewarding, taking you to another level of your relationship with the Lord."

—Bryan Johnson, Senior Pastor,
Revive Covenant Church

Table of Contents

Welcome

If you and I are alike, picking up this book took courage. A purchase like this comes with deep acceptance of the character challenges we face and our need for help. But we take another risk when we crack the cover: we inwardly hope that we won't be disappointed. We don't want the author to tell us what we already know.

Maybe our current understanding of Christian growth brought substantial change in the least stubborn parts of our hearts but sputtered in our more entrenched pockets of troublesome character. When we're encouraged to move past our deep-seated flaws by doing those same things we've already devoted ourselves to, we can feel frustrated and angry or racked with guilt and shame. We've tried! But even our sustained best efforts produced little movement. So now what do we do? Where do we turn for help? Who can we trust for guidance?

You are not alone. Many of us carry unresolved character issues that affect our relationships, quality of life, and witness. Experience has taught us that these parts of our hearts are resistant to growth. But they don't have to be permanent handicaps. Let's work on them together.

We will start with a simple answer to the complex question of problematic character: we need Jesus. But it will take us three months to unpack this answer and build a practical approach to its implementation in the most entrenched parts of our hearts. At the end of our twelve-week journey together, we will not fully resolve the character issue; we will establish ourselves on a hopeful, biblical path toward dramatic transformation. This position alone will begin to change our lives.

Before we jump in, let's consider three points of encouragement that will help us get the most out of this experience:

First, think about asking one or two men to journey with you. God designed us with dependence in mind—dependence on Him and on one another. Experience has taught me how much we need other men in our lives. Looking back over the thirty-two years I've followed Jesus, I can't help but notice that I often got into trouble when I kept my cards close to my chest. On the other hand, safety, strength, and freedom followed my decisions to walk with faithful men in my weaknesses.

Of course, we must choose wisely. Not all potential companions are safe for us. We want to walk with self-aware men, ready to work on their own problem areas, and willing to lend us strength. The fellowship we need on a journey like this is not so much about accountability but mutual support and encouragement. If we need heavy doses of accountability to move through this book, we might not be ready for the experience.

Second, read only one chapter per week and read it twice. Since this is a guidebook, we seek more than information alone. We want a facilitated experience, a guided journey. Journeys take time.

I've had to learn this truth over and over again. My first encounter with the lesson is still with me today. When I was a boy, my Aunt Emma came to town for a visit. The night before her flight home, she noticed a small jewelry box I made for my mom. She loved the size, proportions, and all-wood construction and wanted one just like it. When she left the room, I slipped out to the garage and got to work.

I was in a hurry and frustrated by the time crunch. Within minutes, I shook off my respect for the woodworking skills I had acquired and took a shortcut. My dad noticed the error, and he knew that I would not be happy with the finished product. He stepped up beside me. "You know," he said, "That's not the right way to work that step." I exploded: "I don't have *time* to do it right!" Unfazed, he answered, "You always have time to do it right."

These words have come back to me many times over the years. We can't rush something that, by its nature, takes more time—especially character change. So, let's focus on only one chapter per week and read through the content twice. After the first read, set the book aside for a few days. Then, come back to it and take another look. Once you sense that the content has settled in your mind and heart, you'll be in an excellent position to tackle the prayer project for the week.

Third, try to marinate in the prayer projects. Each chapter includes a prayer exercise to help you engage with God in the week's content. I first encountered prayer projects in seminary, and they helped me address questions with God that I wouldn't have thought to ask. Carve out plenty of unrushed time to interact with the questions in a quiet place where you won't be interrupted. Then, answer each question as honestly as you can. Drop all filters, pay attention to your reactions, and write down the raw truth in a notebook you set aside for this journey. Writing our answers—especially by hand—helps us open our souls to God and own where we are.

Finally, you will notice that I talk about God the Father and God the Son throughout the book, with only periodic mention of God the Holy Spirit. However, the ministry of the Spirit is central to our journey together—the weeks ahead are saturated with His presence and His work. Scripture tells us that He dwells within all of us who believe and that Jesus takes residence in our hearts through the Holy Spirit. When we open more of our heart to Jesus—and when we live and work with Him there—we live and work with the Spirit of Christ.

We're ready now to jump in. Let's begin Week 1.

May God's love and mercy and His peace and kindness go before us and accompany us. Amen.

How Do We Come to Terms with Hidden Pockets of Troublesome Character?

I f we take enough steps back from our journey with God, we might notice that we have walked through different seasons with Him. When I review my relationship with Jesus, I see a remarkable difference, for example, between those early years of our life together and the years that followed. A shift, really.

I gave my life to God when I was twenty-seven, and dramatic change immediately followed. I was excited—I learned new things about Him and His ways all the time and was determined to put my new understanding into practice. My application of knowledge took on many forms, but the dominant expression was "remove and replace." As I started to recognize the sin I carried into my Christian life, I tried to uproot it. Then, I would backfill the hole with something healthier for me and those around me. For example, I pulled up and replanted how I talked, how I spent my time, who I spent my time with, what I read or watched on TV, and my overarching purpose. These changes and many others made me feel more settled and at peace. In a real sense, I was finally home. And I couldn't help but form a conclusion that would have to be shattered down the road: being with Jesus and other believers always feels excellent, and I routinely grow in leaps and bounds. Perfection must be just over the horizon—this is awesome!

Needless to say, I was utterly disoriented when God began to unfold the next season of our journey together. The "onward and upward" trajectory I was flying pitched over and plummeted toward the earth. I stopped growing. Of course, I wondered if this shutdown in development was somehow my fault. So, I ticked through my inventory of spiritual practices. I quickly noticed that I was doing the same things I had done from the start—I still went to church, read my Bible, prayed, participated in a small group study, enjoyed regular worship and fellowship, and served in the church. But now, nothing was happening. Years would pass before I understood what this new season was about: deeper—and much slower—character change.

Now that I have more than three decades of experience with Jesus, as well as seminary training and a long church ministry, I recognize that my shift in seasons was normal and expected. Whenever God feels we're ready—whenever He knows that our foundation with Him is sturdy enough—He will show us some areas of our heart or "rooms in our house" that require special care and transformation.[1]

How did He show you the room or rooms that led you to pick up this book? My guess is that we can't even count the number of ways God reveals deeper truths about our character. However He chooses to do it—whether awareness comes through bogged-down growth as it did with me, through the Word, or through difficulties of various kinds, such as marriage, children, relationship challenges, spiritual dryness and boredom, exhaustion, or something else—we begin to notice troubling parts of our character that are still with us, still hanging on. Our discovery can take us by surprise, especially when we recognize that these problematic pockets are entrenched, strong, and stubborn.

The pocket that concerns us most could be anything: anxiety, fear, worry, anger, lust, insecurity, control, pervasive sadness, jealousy, selfishness, arrogance, people-pleasing, etc. Our inner voice often amplifies our concern and grows critical and demanding: "Why am I still stuck in this area? I must not be doing enough. I need to get more serious about my life with God—I have to try harder." So, we resolve to double down on effort in our spiritual practices and in obedience, hoping to make some encouraging headway. But our surge in effort only leaves our life with God feeling pressurized and burdensome. Our intentional and concentrated push doesn't work.

---

[1] Dr. John Coe, "Introduction to Christian Spirituality and Prayer" (lecture, Talbot School of Theology, La Mirada, CA, 2008).

Now what? Where do we turn for help?

We don't know.

Other men in our church look put together and pretty squared away, so sharing our character challenge with them might feel risky. Instead, we take the safe route and opt out of disclosure. We press on as best we can, going through the motions and trying not to think about what all this might mean.

Bless you, brother, if I have described your current experience. It is hard to walk around with a secret, especially one that constantly threatens to shame us and isolate us. But with compassion, I have to tell you that there are still a couple of high hurdles to clear before we can come to terms with our hidden challenges: *accepting where we are* and *receiving what we hear.*

This sounds straightforward, but fully accepting where we are can provoke many disturbing questions and powerful emotions. We now must weather a storm of possible explanations for our failure to mature in the pocket of character that concerns us. These possibilities stretch far beyond lack of effort and can sometimes be heart-breaking or even terrifying: What if Christianity doesn't work? What if there's something horribly wrong with me? What if God doesn't love or engage with me like He does with others? The waves of questions surge toward us and crash over us, and the force of their weight holds us under.

After the first waves of questions dissipate, we spot others moving toward us: What if this gets out? What will others think of me if they discover my character defect? Will those I love still love me? Will I continue to be accepted in my circle of friends? And maybe the biggest question of all for men: What if I lose the respect of others?

No wonder coming to terms with our flaws requires so much courage. We have to move forward in the face of many fears.

Once the difficult questions lose some of their power, it is time to listen. What is our experience telling us? For some men, our persistent character challenge might be telling us that it *is* time to get more serious about our life with God or that it *is* time to put more effort into our spiritual practices. However, for devoted men, like the man who would pick up this book, our lingering character defect might tell us something very different: It's time to redirect some of our efforts.

For devoted men, lack of seriousness and effort have not been our problems, right? We've been sincere—we have tried hard in study, prayer, and obedience to become more fully the men we were created to be, to put off the old man and put on the new:

> *To put off your old self, which belongs to your former manner of life and is corrupt through deceitful desires, and to be renewed in the spirit of your minds, and to put on the new self, created after the likeness of God in true righteousness and holiness.*
>
> Ephesians 4:22–24

Many of us, especially those of us who are conservative evangelicals, carry out Paul's instructions in Ephesians 4 through a sturdy, two-part approach to spiritual growth:

1. **Leave behind my sinful conduct**. My old behavior is part of my former manner of life. The old has gone, and the new has come. I want to live this truth.
2. **Apply myself toward the vision of the man I want to be.** Think like that man, and act like that man. As I do, the Spirit will enable me to *become* that man.

We seem to have plenty of scriptural basis for this approach to growth. In addition to Ephesians 4, isn't this strategy consistent with Paul's exhortation below?

> *But one thing I do: forgetting what lies behind and straining forward to what lies ahead, I press on toward the goal for the prize of the upward call of God in Christ Jesus.*
>
> Philippians 3:13–14

I unpack these verses in Philippians more fully in my first book. But I will briefly point out what Paul seems to be saying here, then draw a conclusion that will help point the way forward for us.

We want to be careful not to take Paul's action out of context. If we properly seat verses 13 and 14 in the context of his writing throughout Philippians 3, Paul appears to leave behind *his confidence in the flesh*. Remember, he used to be self-reliant. He zealously tried to make himself righteous before God in his own strength and accomplishments. He now leaves behind this dependence on his own power and resumé as he puts his whole weight on Jesus. Therefore, when Paul tells us to put off the old man (Eph. 4:22) or to forget what is behind (Phil. 3:13–14), he doesn't appear to be saying, "Always turn your back to the old man; focus on the new man."

This is good news that probably lines up well with our growth journey. In the least stubborn parts of our old character, the two-part action plan on page eight works well, right? But for our most entrenched character flaws, it often does not. Practically speaking, our strategy compels us to push down these troubled areas, repressing them. Even though we bury them, they do not go away or dissipate. The defects hang on, telling us that we may have gone as far as we can go with our resist-the-old-and-put-on-the-new approach. It's time to redirect some of our efforts away from putting on the new man and apply them toward putting off the most stubborn parts of the old man in a different, more effective way.

I guess some of us feel relief and hope when we hear that there might be a different approach to transformation in the most problematic parts of our character. Others of us, though, may feel resistance. I sure did. No doubt, there could be many reasons why we push back on change. But one stands out to me: *inertia*.

The word *inertia* is a physics term tied to Newton's first law of motion. So, let's check in with NASA for a crisp definition: "An object at rest remains at rest, and an object in motion remains in motion at a constant speed and in a straight line unless acted on by an unbalanced force."[2]

We can safely substitute the word *soul* for *object* in this explanation. Most of us don't seem to have the time, energy, or impetus for change. We tend to believe—or we want to believe—that we understand what

---

[2] "Newton's Laws of Motion," Glenn Research Center, NASA, August 7, 2023, https://www1.grc.nasa.gov/beginners-guide-to-aeronautics/newtons-laws-of-motion/.

we need to know and apply our knowledge appropriately, even in the complex area of transformation. Simply put, we tend to stay as we are.

Underneath this fixed disposition, a secret desire may mislead us: we want growth on our terms. And, hey, why wouldn't we? I routinely bump into the part of myself that is committed to my comfort. This protective side is a master builder of blind spots. Impressive, really. I need others who don't mind sharing their opinions on matters close to my heart. Without them, only God knows what I would convince myself of.

To overcome inertia, we will likely need a couple of things: first, an unbalanced force strong enough to move us in a new direction, and second, a willingness to make space in our lives for a more profound journey with Jesus. We'll discuss the former next week when we explore the next logical question in our conversation: What happens if we decide to keep these stubborn pockets out of sight? There are significant consequences when we submerge parts of our hearts. The surprising truth about repression might give us the push we need. The latter—making space in our lives for a deeper journey with Jesus—is part of the prayer project below. Most of us employ a variety of distractions to occupy ourselves and draw attention away from matters of the heart. My favorite is productivity—I love to stay busy with things that push different parts of my life forward while helping others. So, something has to give. Although I try to occupy myself with good things, I must create space for what is best.

Okay, we're ready for our first prayer project. As discussed in the Welcome section, try to set aside plenty of unrushed time to sit with God and mull over these questions with Him. Finding a quiet place where you won't be disturbed is best. Answer each question as honestly as you can. Writing down your answers in a notebook reserved for this experience is also helpful. Writing, especially by hand, helps us see and accept what comes up in these prayer times.

Prayer Project

1. Take another look at the standard, two-part approach to spiritual growth on page eight. How well does this strategy describe your beliefs about Christian character development? What would you add or subtract? Why?

2. Spend some time talking with God about growth. In what areas of your life have you seen significant change? What areas seem resistant to change?

3. What do you do with the most stubborn parts of your old character? How well does the approach work for you?

4. Ask the Lord, "Am I willing to make space in my life to address one of these character challenges in a different way with you?" Why or why not?

Week 2

What Happens if
We Choose to Keep
These Stubborn Pockets Out
of Sight?

You've probably heard the saying, "There's more going on here than meets the eye." The old adage rings true with repression. We rarely see the far-reaching impacts of buried character flaws. Therefore, if we are debating whether or not to address one of these hidden defects, we should explore the potential consequences of choosing not to.

So, what happens when we keep stubborn pockets of troublesome character out of sight?

Nothing good.

I say this with a heavy sigh. We pay a high price for repression, and I'm afraid those around us do, too. So, let's unpack this two-word answer and better understand the nature of repression and its costs. Two more questions logically flow from our question of the week:

1. What happens to the stuff we push down?
2. What does it do to us?

What happens to this stuff we push down?

We should take a moment to acknowledge that our ability to suppress parts of our hearts is not all bad. I can think of instances when I was grateful for the God-given ability to block out experiences and emotions that were too much for me to handle at the time. I'm sure there will be more occurrences in the future as well. Eventually, however, we must go back and deal with *some* of our lost parts. Here's why: the experiences and emotions we block out remain pristine. Their power does not diminish over time; they are as pure and raw as the moment we first repressed them. Our goal in bottling these powerful emotions was to *stop feeling them*. Of course, we didn't foresee that capping the bottle would also preserve them. Re-encountering these parts of our hearts is like traveling back in time.

I flew to Washington state in the winter of 2012, where my time machine was prepped and waiting for me—an enormous house overlooking Puget Sound. I drove from Seattle's airport late in the afternoon on a Saturday and swung by the grocery store to pick up enough food to last the three-week journey I was about to embark on. It was early evening when I finally turned up the long, gradual slope leading to the impressive-looking capsule that would take me back to who knows where. I wasted no time—I had a schedule to keep. My seminary program allotted a firm twenty-one days for this experience. So, once I put away my food and unpacked, I strapped myself into the only seat facing a large dashboard with a single green button labeled "GO."

I took a deep breath and slowly released it. I nervously adjusted my position in the seat. Then, I leaned forward and pressed the button.

My three-week retreat was underway. You've probably guessed that this was no ordinary retreat. I was utterly alone in the expansive home. No host or hostess was there to serve me or whisk me off to well-planned and entertaining diversions. In fact, there were no distractions of any kind—no phone, computer, television, or music. No books, games, or hobbies. Nothing except my Bible, pen, and paper. Even my physical activity was restricted. I could take slow walks in the countryside, but I was prohibited from strenuous work or exercise that could dissipate pent-up emotions more quickly than I could pay attention to them. Fortunately, I did have a guide for the journey—a Christian psychologist who met with me for ninety minutes every weekday morning before sunup. Super appealing, right?

The goal of my getaway was to isolate myself in deep silence with God so that some of my heart's repressed parts could bubble into view. And wow—they did. I was forty-seven years old then, and life afforded me plenty of opportunities to push down many things. Who knew which part of my heart would show itself first? I got my answer within the first couple of days; I began to see the reasons for my depression.

For years, I felt flat and heavy, like I was only partially alive and weighed two times what the bathroom scale reflected back to me. I had grown used to feeling depressed; it was normal and familiar to me, so I wasn't always aware of my problem. However, when I came across Jesus's words in verses like John 10:10 or John 15:10-11, the reality of my inner life slammed into me:

I came that they may have life and have it abundantly.

John 10:10

These things I have spoken to you, that my joy may be in you, and that your joy may be full.

John 15:11

Where was my joy? What happened to the promise of abundant life? These questions haunted me until I felt compelled to seek answers with Jesus.

In the solitude and silence of the retreat house, the answers began to emerge from the depths of my heart. Potent memories started to bubble up, piece by piece, and take on their original shapes. The emotions that went with them gradually made their appearance as well, swelling inside me and threatening to erupt like a spewing volcano. First, anger. Not garden-variety anger—what I experienced was more akin to rage. Its power shocked and rattled me. As my anger continued to build, I felt the impulse to shred everything in sight. I told my retreat director that I was worried I might tear down the house, and I meant it. He didn't seem too bothered, though. Calmy, he addressed my concerns:

Director: "How much money do you have?"
Me: "A good bit."

Director: "Pay for whatever you ruin. But don't hurt yourself."
Me: "Uh … Copy that."

As I walked out the door to return to the house, he mentioned that our anger often feels overwhelming, even infinite. But it is finite. "You'll be okay," he said. I needed to hear that.

God and I returned to the house that morning and cut loose my emotions. My fury flooded the residence, both verbally and through pounding away at objects that wouldn't hurt my hands but still gave me the sensation of laying into something substantial. Several intense sessions like this followed until my rage had finally spent itself. I sat on the floor, exhausted, sweaty, and panting for air. Sometime later, I lifted my eyes and surveyed the massive living room. I had destroyed only one piece of furniture. "Excellent," I thought. "I won't have to settle up for much."

Less than a day or so later, something underneath the anger made its way to the surface: pain and profound sadness. I later learned that anger often covers deep wounds. This rule of thumb proved true in my case. Heartache engulfed me, and again, God and I resolved to let it be what it was. If anybody had peered through the windows that week, they would've been alarmed to see a grown man crying as hard as a small child. The spigots were wide open. But, like my anger, the tears couldn't last forever. Eventually, they exhausted themselves.

I felt like I had awakened in a different world. I was much more present in the moment and in everything around me. God and I sat together or went for leisurely walks in deep peace and surprising clarity. It was day nineteen. We had spent the fuel that powered my depression by allowing stored memories and emotions to rise to the surface and be what they were. I secured a new lease on life and am grateful beyond words.

I came away from the retreat with first-hand knowledge that shaped part of my future ministry. Whatever we repress—both the uncomfortable emotions and the experiences connected to them—remains as pure and raw as the moment we first separated ourselves from it. In Washington, I relived some of those earlier times with God. He and I went back together, and His presence, compassion, truth, love, and guidance brought a lot of health and vitality to those closed-off parts of myself. He raised me more fully to life as the man He created me to be.

Fortunately, we don't need to launch into a radical retreat or tear something apart to find healing and growth in troubled parts of our character. My seminary training required an accelerated process so I could help others after I graduated without adding a significant, unresolved character issue to the mix. For most of us, though, our lives and responsibilities demand a longer and more gradual process. This guidebook aims to help us enter into that process of deeper, life-changing growth.

What does it do to us?

Now we know that the stuff we push down doesn't go away. So, it's time to understand how these buried parts of our hearts might affect us. It shouldn't be a big deal, right? Out of sight, out of mind?

Not exactly.

I already mentioned that my suppression popped up as depression. Since I'm not a psychologist, I am in no position to identify other psychological maladies that might arise from blocking off various parts of our hearts. But I will highlight some general costs of "doing business" this way.

Those of us who invest in the stock market know the golden strategy—buy low and sell high. We don't want to sell our shares for less than we paid for them. If we do sell when the stock price drops, we lock in our losses. Similarly, if we ignore the parts of our heart we have repressed, we lock in our losses. We'll spend the rest of the chapter looking at five of these costly impacts.

- **Stunted growth**. The parts of our hearts that we bury out of sight do not develop. They don't grow. As you saw in the first half of this chapter, these trouble spots are frozen in time. Unfortunately, they are also highly resistant to any indirect attempts at change, such as striving to overcome them through opposite thinking and behavior or asking God to take them away. So, even though we may be high-functioning men with a lot of responsibility, the buried parts of our hearts leave us with a sense that something is wrong. For example, we might feel washed out inside, needing more substance, solidness, and sturdiness. Or, we may notice that we are encumbered as if we were running with a drag chute trailing behind us. Some of us could feel like posers, as I once did—we sense that we don't measure up to manhood's requirements, and we are more comfortable identifying ourselves as "guys" rather than men. Others of us wish we were more adventurous, spontaneous, or creative. Regardless of how we experience the influence of our repressed hearts, the locked pockets of troublesome character limit our growth and leave us wanting.

- **Conforming life.**[3] Hidden places in our hearts can heavily influence our lives and relationships by secretly directing our values, attitudes, and behavior. We might adopt a distorted view of masculinity that conforms to the experiences and emotions we have buried. If we harbor anger, for example, we may value an excessively strong concept of manhood. Qualities like honesty, directness, decisiveness, and firmness rise to the status of false virtues. While these attributes in themselves are honorable, they now supersede love. We have weaponized the attributes, making ourselves overbearing, demanding, impatient, harsh, or bullies.

- **Reactive life.**[4] On the other hand, we may abhor the emotions we have buried and embrace a different distortion of masculinity altogether. Staying with our example of anger, we may react against our outrage and adopt an overly gentle concept of manhood. Patience, kindness, compassion, and tolerance become our false virtues. Again, what makes these otherwise noble qualities false is their position above love. By elevating these qualities higher than love, we have cast off our responsibility to love others more truthfully and proactively, especially when speaking out is difficult and unpopular. We become passive men. I landed in this

---

[3] Based on my understanding of Dr. Karen Horney's work: Horney, Neurosis and Human Growth, W. W. Norton & Company, Inc., New York, 1950, Pages 17-23.

[4] Horney, Neurosis and Human Growth, W. W. Norton & Company, Inc., New York, 1950, Pages 17-23.

category in the past. I harbored anger, but I was also a people-pleaser. The tension I experienced in this duality didn't make life much fun.

- **Fearfulness**. We bury memories and emotions because we're afraid of them. We don't believe we can handle the turmoil they might cause. Typically, we don't want these parts of our hearts running loose in front of others, either. What would happen if they leaked out? Would those who caught sight of these character issues still accept us? Could we still be loved and respected? Maintaining a safe distance from damaging leakage becomes a high priority, and we turn to heightened vigilance and control to maintain safe borders. We keep people at a distance. We don't engage in activities that might threaten exposure. Consequently, we are smaller than God made us to be. Our lives are smaller. This is heartbreaking. I forfeited so much of my life by protecting myself from improbable outcomes.

- **Compromised witness**. Sometimes, answers to big questions are shockingly—and uncomfortably—simple. When asked about the cause of so much poverty in the world, Mother Theresa said, "We don't share."[5] Similarly, many people today recognize the reason for the decline in our Western church: *We aren't different enough*. I'm sure there are numerous explanations for this lack of distinction and plans to address the problem. But I want to identify a center of gravity (COG) to target. A COG denotes the single action I can take that would significantly impact my situation. In military terms, we might identify a center of gravity by answering this question: "If I had only one bomb to drop, where would I drop it if I wanted to cause the most direct and indirect damage?" In our church context, our question might be, "If the world needs to see Christian men who are remarkably different—who are authentic and radically transformed—what single action could we take to move us forward the farthest?" Many of the actions we currently take are very good, like Scripture study, obedience, worship, community life, and meaningful

---

[5] Mother Theresa, directed by Ann Petrie and Jeanette Petrie (1986; New York City, NY: Petrie Productions), DVD.

service to one another and our communities. I believe that if we could also deal directly and honestly with God in the hidden places of our hearts, we would change our lives and witness in the most dramatic and attractive ways.

As we wind up this chapter and move into our prayer project for the week, let's take a step back from the five losses we've just discussed and ask ourselves: What do they seem to have in common? Our *quality of life* is definitely a common denominator. But, perhaps more prominently, these losses significantly impact *relationships*. Our relationships suffer when we stuff down pockets of troublesome character because we are left with a diminished ability to trust and to love robustly and well. We all know the greatest commandment:

You shall love the Lord your God with all your heart and with all your soul and with all your mind. This is the great and first commandment. And a second is like it: You shall love your neighbor as yourself. On these two commandments depend all the Law and the Prophets.

Matthew 22:37–40

It follows that we must address the parts of our hearts that hold us back from a deeper experience of God's love and its free expression to Him and others. More on this later in the book.

After reading this week's content, I realize we might feel deflated. There wasn't a pile of good news. Help is on the way. Over the next two weeks, we will unpack our current understanding of growth and discuss God's view of our repressed hearts. I believe the chapters will strengthen and encourage you. In the meantime, please work through the prayer project below as honestly as possible.

Prayer Project

1. Ask yourself and ask God, "Where did I see myself in this chapter? What parts of the discussion were like looking into a mirror?"

2. Spend unhurried time with God in each part of the chapter that rang deep and true. What is your reaction to these

reflections? Do you feel seen? Relieved? Exposed? Afraid? Talk with Jesus about this.

3. Where are you now with Question 4 from last week's prayer project? Do you find yourself more willing to make space to address one of your character challenges? Not so much? Why?

4. Sit quietly with God and let this question hang in the air: "Lord, what do You want to show me?"

Our Current Understanding of Growth

I wish we could sit together and talk for a while. I would love to know how you're doing after last week's prayer project. What did you see? How do you feel about it? What are your intentions going forward?

Maybe you are more convinced than ever that you must face a troublesome part of your heart with Jesus. If so, we should take the next step in our journey together. Let's identify and unpack our current understanding of growth. We need to know what we believe about character change before we make any adjustments.

Let's go back to Ephesians:

> *To put off your old self, which belongs to your former manner of life and is corrupt through deceitful desires, and to be renewed in the spirit of your minds, and to put on the new self, created after the likeness of God in true righteousness and holiness.*
>
> Ephesians 4:22-24 (emphasis mine)

In Week 1, we highlighted a two-part course of action that many of us follow to execute these commands:

1. **Leave behind my sinful conduct**. My old behavior is part of my former manner of life. The old has gone, and the new has come. I want to live this truth.

2. **Apply myself toward the vision of the man I want to be**. Think like that man, and act like that man. As I do, the Spirit will enable me to *become* that man.

I'm not sure if someone taught me this simple plan. I don't remember a discipleship course that so succinctly outlined my responsibility for transformation. But this two-part approach to maturation somehow got into my system, and it seemed to match up well with Paul's call to action in Ephesians. I grew a lot.

Here's where it got tricky: I didn't realize that I carried some deep beliefs about discipleship to Jesus that would someday stall my spiritual growth and leave me exhausted. I uncovered these core values one morning when I first recognized that I wasn't moving forward. Concerned and in the mood for self-reflection, I reviewed my understanding of character change and pinpointed my problem. I'm glad I sat down. I was determined to get to the root of the matter, and my investigation took a while.

Many of us have a hard time outlining our view of sanctification. After all, we may not have been taught how to grow; we "caught" how to grow. If our church's understanding of Christian development wasn't explicitly stated, it was still in the mix—everywhere. A theology of growth was woven into the pastor's preaching, ministries of the church, exhortations from fellow congregants, and the books we read. Beliefs and instructions about transformation were in the air we breathed. We just absorbed them.

As I sat at my kitchen table and sifted through my thoughts, I was surprised to find four sturdy beliefs driving all my efforts to change. My surprise was not at discovering these convictions but how they felt. They seemed matter-of-fact and well-established like they had been firmly in place for years, even though I had never articulated them. Here's what I wrote down:

- I should be grateful for what Jesus did for me when He died on the cross.

- I should express my gratitude through obedience to God's Word. I should be the kind of man He wants me to be and live the set-apart life He wants me to live.

- I should work diligently in my spiritual practices (Bible reading, prayer, worship, service, etc.) and try to obey God in all things. As I do, the Holy Spirit will subtly change me inside to align my character with my outward actions and make me the kind of man who walks in the fruit of the Spirit.

- I should change more when I put more effort into my spiritual practices, particularly obedience.

After metabolizing the shock I felt, I resolved right then and there to do the only thing I could do to push ahead: try harder. My understanding of growth offered no explanation for my stalled development other than my lack of gratitude and effort. So, I had no choice—I would mount a considerable and sustained surge to bridge my labor gap and demonstrate genuine gratitude. I wasted little time. I launched into the future with a clear plan and a zero percent chance of success.

What about you? Do these four "shoulds" seem to echo your experience as well? I'm pretty sure I'm not alone. I've seen plenty of affirmative head nods when I've shared this belief system with devoted brothers. But any list of "shoulds" must rest on assumptions. So, let's take a moment to look through the four points again. What suppositions might be supporting our list?

I think there are two:

1. It's all up to us. Our personal determination dictates our progress, right? Suppose we study enough to understand what we are to be like, work hard enough to obey, and persist long enough. In that case, the change agent is further released inside of us to secretly align our character with our outward actions and make us better men. We will steadily become men with a character like Jesus's character. Well, this was my former understanding, anyway.

I remember the opening weeks of my very first class in seminary. The professor, Dr. John Coe, wrote a lot on the whiteboard. I'm a visual learner, so I was in my natural habitat when he cluttered the board with diagrams, key points, and arrows racing in all directions. One afternoon, he was on a roll—as he almost always was—when he dropped this little nugget: "We believe that we control our own growth."[6] I felt like I

---

[6] Dr. John Coe, "Introduction to Christian Spirituality and Prayer" (lecture, Talbot School of Theology, La Mirada, CA, 2008).

was in a dream. I lost awareness of the thirty-five other students in the classroom. Only Dr. Coe and I were there. He seemed to know and understand my story—he spoke directly to me and my four deep beliefs. His conclusion was earth-shaking: I had embraced a cause-and-effect spirituality. "If I do *this*, then God does *that* proportionately," I believed. I had placed the entire weight of Christian development on my own shoulders and—unknowingly—shut down a deeper, more transformative relationship with Jesus. Dr. Coe launched my seminary training by causing the ground to collapse beneath me.

While this new consciousness was disturbing and disorienting, there were a couple of encouraging elements. When I regained awareness of my classmates, their facial expressions told me I was not the only one falling through the floor. The fact that our professor lectured on cause-and-effect Christian living so early in our seminary careers was even more soothing evidence that I suffered from a common misunderstanding. It's a relief to know that we are not alone.

As the semester wore on, I finally understood why I felt stuck in a lose-lose way of life. When I managed to gain some degree of mastery over a troublesome aspect of my character, I correspondingly lost ground to arrogance and judgmentalism. I got puffy. Hey, if growth is up to me, why shouldn't I pat myself on the back after a successful campaign? Secretly, I felt that I was better than others who struggled the same way I used to. "I can do it, and you cannot," I would think in the safety of my own mind. In the end, I hijacked whatever progress I made in the faith. My efforts did not bring more freedom to love well. I only found a new way to elevate myself above others in my never-ending quest to feel superior. On the other hand, if my efforts to change some part of my life proved unsuccessful, my inner voice spoke differently: "Others can do this, but I cannot." These words easily crushed me under the weight of guilt and shame.

2. We do not have to engage with the stubborn parts of our old character to be transformed. Direct encounters with pockets of stubborn character are unnecessary now. This is welcome news, isn't it? We don't have to deal with the problematic parts of our hearts that we want nothing to do with anyway. We just have to outrun them and maybe employ a stiff-

arm occasionally. After all, we're racing for the endzone—it wouldn't be helpful to get dragged down behind the line of scrimmage. So, over time, we come to see troublesome places in our repressed hearts as internal adversaries bent on crippling any serious attempts we make to put on the new man. Even more, these inner opponents threaten added pain and humiliation through their power to grind us down in failure, guilt, and shame. Unsurprisingly, we abhor direct encounters and embrace a theology of growth that renders contact needless or even dangerous.

These two assumptions play out in our lives with staggering consequences. The most stubborn parts of our old character remain with us, and they stand firm. No surge in effort can dislodge them and secure their cooperation in our character improvement project. And God hasn't taken them away. Left without energy or options, we do whatever we can to hide our character flaws. The costly impacts of repression we identified in Chapter Two become a way of life.

No wonder we hear about brothers in church leadership being overtaken by powerful pockets of troubled character. It actually makes sense, doesn't it? The repressed parts of our hearts lurk beneath the surface of our lives. Given the right set of circumstances, they could break out and carry the day. It could happen to any of us. It has certainly happened to me.

But is this all there is? Do we spend the rest of our days trapped in a no-growth zone? Where is the love, joy, and abundant life we hoped for and worked hard for?

Good news—there is so much more for us than we have experienced. Paul seems to concentrate a lot on our personal responsibility in transformation. And solid effort is required on our part, no doubt. But he does not push the idea that our growth is entirely on us or that we never have to deal directly with pockets of entrenched character flaws. As a whole, Scripture testifies to something very different: transformation comes through God's power, and we partner with Him to see change happen. Even—and especially—in the most stubborn regions of our hearts.

Next week, we will examine God's intentions toward us in our sanctification journey. Until then, please spend plenty of unhurried time with Him in the prayer project below.

Prayer Project

1. What has your sanctification journey been like for you? Has growth been a life-giving partnership between you and Jesus? Has it been confusing, pressurized, or burdensome? Talk with Jesus about this.

2. How well do the two assumptions about growth in this chapter match your beliefs about Christian character development? Would you add or subtract anything? Why?

3. Where does this week leave you? Are you discouraged? Hopeful? Why?

4. Check with God about the disposition of your soul moving ahead to Week 4. Are you open and willing to hear more? Do you feel cautious and reserved? Talk with Him about this.

Week 4

What Are God's Intentions Toward Us in the Problematic Parts of Our Characters?

S o far in our journey together, we have examined our personal views and experiences of Christian growth, particularly in the most problematic parts of our characters. Now, we want to step outside ourselves as best we can and look at God's view of our character issues and how He might want to address them. Suppose we compare and contrast our perspectives and approaches with His. With an honest review of how we do not align, we can redirect some of our efforts to cooperate more fully with Him.

Scripture tells us that God intends to transform even our most stubborn pockets of troublesome character. This is good news, right? He also seems to require our cooperation in this work, which probably comes as no surprise. However, to partner with God, we need to do something that might feel uncomfortable or even disorienting. We must reverse our two assumptions about spiritual growth:

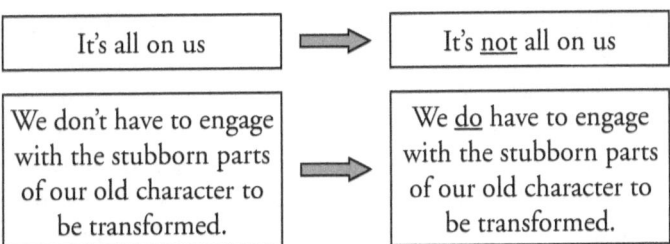

It's all on us	➡	It's <u>not</u> all on us
We don't have to engage with the stubborn parts of our old character to be transformed.	➡	We <u>do</u> have to engage with the stubborn parts of our old character to be transformed.

Suppose you're responding to this reversal the way I first did. In that case, you might feel relieved that you are not in charge of your growth but troubled by the idea that you must deal directly with disturbing character flaws. No worries. We'll spend the rest of our time this week discussing these new assumptions.

It's not all on us.

Romans offers a great starting place for our conversation:

> *And we know that for those who love God all things work together for good, for those who are called according to his purpose. For those whom he foreknew he also predestined to be conformed to the image of His Son, in order that he might be the firstborn among many brothers.*

Romans 8:28–29

From these verses, we see that God works in all things for our benefit, above all our transformation. He decided long ago that *He* would do this work—he would take our character, no matter how contorted, and reshape it to reflect the form of Jesus's character. Thankfully, God always works to make us more loving, joyful, peaceable, patient, kind, good, faithful, gentle, and self-controlled (Gal. 5:22–23). These fruits of the Spirit are not mere behavioral changes but the natural outflow of a changed heart. We don't just act differently than we used to—we become *different men* simply being ourselves.

Now, we begin to see even more of the tragedy of repression. When we bury the parts of our character that refused to come with us when we chose to put on the new man, we cut them off. This violent action terminates so much growth potential. Dr. John Coe explained it this way: our suppressed hearts hold vital human capacities.[7] Unfortunately, these capacities have been formed into problematic character. Our malformed character must be reformed into righteous character. For example, if I have an anger problem, I don't deny that my capacity for anger is good. God made me in His image, and He sometimes gets angry. But my capacity for anger has been poorly formed—I am an angry man susceptible to improper conduct. My anger must be

---

[7] Dr. John Coe, "Christian Virtue and the Spiritual Disciplines." (lecture, Talbot School of Theology, La Mirada, CA, 2009).

reformed into appropriate anger. If I repress my entrenched character problem, I shut down all hope for reformation on this side of a personal crisis that might compel me to adequately address the issue.

Peace to you, brother, if this is a heart-wrenching perspective. Rest in the assurances God gives us in Romans 8:28–29. He will meet you, and He will do the work of transformation. All you need to know now is your part in it.

We do have to engage with the stubborn parts of our old character to be transformed.

To better understand what cooperation looks like in God's character renovation, let's take a look at Jesus's teaching in John 15:

> *Abide in me, and I in you. As the branch cannot bear fruit by itself, unless it abides in the vine, neither can you, unless you abide in me. I am the vine; you are the branches. Whoever abides in me and I in him, he it is that bears much fruit, for apart from me you can do nothing.*
>
> John 15:4–5

Here, Jesus confirms that He will cause us to bear fruit. Our part is to abide in Him. He commands us to make our home in Him as the branch makes its home in the vine. He, in turn, makes His home in us.

This "home" language also appears earlier in the Gospel of John. Jesus makes a stunning promise:

> *If anyone loves me, he will keep my word, and my Father will love him, and <u>we will come to him and make our home with him.</u>*
>
> John 14:23 (Emphasis mine)

We know that when we belong to Jesus, He dwells within us through the Holy Spirit. But let's be more descriptive of our radical living arrangement. Like many believers, I used to say, "Jesus lives in me." I was correct, of course. However, John 14:23 depicts our life together much more thoroughly than my description. After trying to get my head around this verse for years, I now say, "Jesus and I live together in me." Do you sense a difference between my former and latter portrayals? When I said, "Jesus lives in me," my interior relationship with Him felt distant and impersonal. I believed He was in me—somewhere—doing whatever He does independently of my awareness, involvement, or, frankly, my concern. This imagined arrangement was only part of a much bigger truth.

Does Jesus want to live within us as if we share a loving home? John 14:23 says, "Yes." It looks like our Sunday School teachers were right after all. If you went to church when you were young, you might remember hearing that our hearts are like large houses with many rooms. I attended Sunday School only a handful of times, but I picked up the "house" metaphor in class, and it stuck with me. "We live together with Jesus in our shared home," our teacher said. "But not in every room." She went on to say that we keep the doors to some rooms closed. Bolted shut. We try not to go near these secret chambers—we wish they were not part of our homes. These places inside hold the most entrenched, complex, and worrisome elements of our character.

It's not surprising that sealed-off rooms are part of our homes. And we probably wouldn't be shocked to learn that God doesn't want to see these parts of our hearts isolated and alone. He desires to be with us in these places, right? So, what would stop us from inviting Him in?

Resolving inhibitors to being with Jesus in once-hidden rooms

Let's set aside personal reasons for our isolation until Week 7. First, we need to address theological reasons. I have two that I'll highlight and unpack in a moment. Before we dive into them, though, I want to underscore a significant point: both reasons led me to the same conclusion. I deduced that I had to get my rooms in order before Jesus could live in them with me. I probably didn't get to this landing place on my own. I've spoken with many devoted men who hold this conclusion as well. But if we feel we must clean up our acts before Jesus can live with us in a problem area, we've put ourselves in a terrible fix. Most of us have failed to get our hidden rooms in order. Seeing no other options, what are we to do but bury the diseased parts of our character and do our best to manage their symptoms?

This is a complicated way to live, but we no longer need to follow this course of action. Let's examine my two theological reasons for blocking Jesus's movements toward my secret rooms. If these reasons are flawed, then my conclusion is suspect. I may not have to wait any longer before I invite Jesus to live with me in a troublesome part of my character.

1. "I'm not supposed to be this way." This conclusion fell out of my misunderstanding of the following verse:

Therefore, if anyone is in Christ, he is a new creation. The old has passed away; behold, the new is come.

2 Corinthians 5:17

With this verse at the forefront of my mind, I felt paralyzed. How could I invite Jesus into an old room that was not supposed to be there anymore? It should have passed away. If He and I open the door to that space now, I'll have to endure a painful tsunami of condemnation, guilt, and shame—not an attractive idea. My theology stipulated that Jesus could be with me in the new parts of our home but not in the old. If I had a room called "Excessive Worry," for example, I could try to tear out the room or do some serious renovations on my own. But I couldn't ask Jesus to be with me in that raw and turbulent space.

I missed the forest for the trees. I didn't fully realize that I *was* a new creation, that the old *had* passed away and the new *had* come. I was a regenerated man, a son of God. I was no longer alone inside—Jesus lived with me there. We walked together in a different world, the Kingdom of God. Jesus knew that not every part of my heart belonged to Him after He sealed me for eternal life with Him. We would deal with those character issues later in my life-long sanctification journey.

So, when we see old places inside that have not yet been made new, our reasonable and best response can be, "Oh. Of course." We're not surprised anymore—we realize that we just haven't gotten there yet. When the time is right, we can go there with Jesus. However, we can go there with Him only if Jesus can be in the presence of our sinful character, right? But is this possible? We'll turn our attention to this question now as we look at the second theological reason I had for locking Jesus out of my hidden rooms.

2. "God is holy—He cannot look upon sin." This conclusion came from many sources, but the weightiest was in Habakkuk:

You who are of purer eyes than to see evil and cannot look at wrong, why do you idly look at traitors and remain silent when the wicked swallows up the man more righteous than he?

Habakkuk 1:13

This verse appears to be compelling evidence that God cannot look upon sin. And if He can't look at my sin, He certainly won't live with me in a room piled with it. Or will He? I unpacked Habakkuk 1:13 in the appendix to my first book, so let's review what I discovered.[8]

Habakkuk 1:13 is part of the prophet's complaint to God that wicked men seem to prosper and go unpunished. In the original language, Hebrew, the word he uses for *see* and the word he uses for *look* have something in common—the element of favor or approval. Another way to look at the verse, then, would be something like this:

"You who are of purer eyes than to approvingly behold evil and cannot look with favor at wrong, why do you idly regard traitors and remain silent when the wicked swallows up the man more righteous than he?"

Habakkuk's complaint is that God seemed to be doing what His character should not allow Him to do: look upon sin with favor, approval, or regard. Habakkuk was incredulous that God remained silent and did not punish the men who abused His people. And he correlated silence and inaction with favor or approval. God answers his complaint by assuring him that retribution will come at its appointed time.

In addition to this corrected understanding of Habakkuk 1:13, we have Jesus's ministry to consider. How did the Lord deal with sin when He was among us? He seemed to move straight toward it. Coming to live among us put Him right in the middle of everything; He must have seen sin all around Him every day. And He moved toward, not away, from those caught in its power. He spent time with sinners (Matt.

---

[8] Joe Storr, The Courage to Be Weak (Fullerton, CA: Asio Creative, 2020) 156–57.

9:11), and He told His disciples that the sick were the ones who needed a physician (Matt. 9:12–13).

God is not threatened by sin; His holiness and integrity are never at risk in the presence of transgression. Surprisingly, He allowed Satan—the father of sin—to speak to Him concerning Job (Job 2:1–8). He is altogether "other" and forever will be. However, it is important to remember that sin cannot remain unchanged in God's presence. Rather, His presence exposes sin (Isa. 6:5) and eradicates it (Heb. 12:29).

We've come a long way in this chapter, haven't we? I hope you feel settled in the knowledge that our spiritual growth is not on us alone. It is God's work. But Jesus commands us to cooperate in this work. He instructs us to abide in Him. We also recognize that our enduring life with Jesus in our shared home involves expanding our living space into once-hidden rooms. Mercifully, He doesn't require us to fix the problems in these rooms before we invite Him in. He asks only that we recognize our need for Him.

Next week, we'll update our understanding of growth from Week 3 and prepare ourselves for the rest of our journey through this guidebook. Until then, allow your hearts to relax and unfold with God in the questions below. Peace to you, brother.

Prayer Project

1. What is your reaction to this statement: "Spiritual growth is not all on you"? What causes you to feel this way?

2. What is your reaction to this statement: "You have to engage with the most stubborn parts of your old character to see them transformed"? What causes you to feel this way?

3. What do you think about asking Jesus to be with you in a particular area of unresolved sin? What comes up for you? Talk with Jesus about this.

4. Sit quietly with God for a while and meditate on this thought: "Apart from You, I can do nothing. Jesus, I need You."

Week 5

What Needs to Change?

I heard a respected engineer say that the best solution to a problem is often the most obvious. His rule of thumb appears to hold true in our case. When we step back and examine our former understanding of growth—placed side-by-side with God's intentions toward us in our repressed character problems—we notice a fundamental disconnect between the two. We tend to distance ourselves from trouble spots while God intends to be with us in them. We must correct our approach to Christian development in our stubborn pockets of troublesome character to eliminate the break. As it turns out, the correction we need aligns us with God's intentions and mirrors the deepest cry of our hearts. "Together with Jesus and not alone" is the life we ache for, even if we're unaware of our yearning.

The diagram below lays out our correction in its simplest form. It enables us to see the root of our past difficulties more clearly. We have been alone and profoundly stuck in the most disturbed places of our hearts. We need to be with Jesus there.

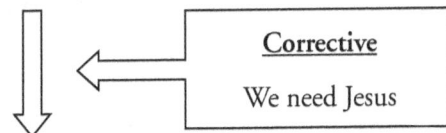

> **Former Understanding of Growth**
>
> left us isolated, alone, and powerless in our entrenched character flaws

> **Corrective**
>
> We need Jesus

> **New Understanding of Growth**
>
> We are together with Jesus in our entrenched character flaws

This new understanding requires us to redirect some of our existing efforts. We've spent enough time and energy trying to keep our distance from the change-resistant parts of our hearts while we work hard to put on the new man. We need to learn how to live with Jesus in these abandoned rooms.

Amazing, isn't it? Jesus wants to co-inhabit troublesome spaces with us. He wants to "do life" with us there. He intends to reshape our problematic character through shared experience and relational work:

> *Come to me, all who labor and are heavy laden, and I will give you rest. Take my yoke upon you, and learn from me, for I am gentle and lowly in heart, and you will find rest for your souls. For my yoke is easy, and my burden is light.*

> Matthew 11:28–30

We can exhale. Our lonely fight for change in the immovable places of our hearts is over. From here on out, we can lean into Jesus.

Let's update our former understanding of growth to align our efforts more closely with God's intentions in our hidden rooms:

- We are dependent on Jesus for growth (John 15:5).
- Our primary effort in this developmental process is to abide in— and with—Jesus. We work in our spiritual exercises to open our hearts/homes to Him and live with Him in reality (John 14:23).
- Our secondary effort is to labor relationally with Jesus and under His leadership to re-form pockets of troubled character and grow in Christ-like character (Rom. 8:28–29, Eph. 4:22–24). We do not have to clean up these rooms before we invite Jesus to be with us in them.

As you can see, this updated path toward maturity still demands significant effort, but we apply ourselves relationally. We work to be in reality with God and follow His leading.

At the same time, we don't want to see Jesus as a means to an end. Our aim in opening troubled places of our hearts is not a resolution of the issues they contain. Our goal is to be with Jesus there. Everything else will take care of itself. Change *will* come. It must come—He is with us, and things change in His presence, acceptance, truth, and love. But we cannot experience all that Jesus is to us if we rush to fix our problems. We miss so much of Him when we move quickly to relieve our distress. Let's start with His presence and allow Him to lead us from there, as He knows best.

I learned firsthand how life-changing it is to be with Jesus in a character trouble spot when I invited Him into one of my most vexing secret rooms. In the spring of 2009, I was on a personal retreat in the San Gabriel Mountains overlooking the southern tip of California's Mojave Desert. I wanted to get far enough away from home to recover some perspective on my life. Mission accomplished—over two days in solitude and silence, I became aware of numerous fears in the depths of my heart. I remember two things about my discovery that surprised me. One, my fears did not orbit around one or two aspects of life. They seemed to be everywhere. As I wrote down my concrete worries, each occupied a different category. I was anxious about my life's purpose, risks I contemplated, finances, health, relationships, ministry, how effectively I used my time, where responsibility was mine and where it was God's, and nearly everything else you can imagine. I felt like I was caught in an avalanche, which led me to fear even my fear.

The second thing that surprised me was this: so little had changed since I launched my long assault on fear. Years earlier, I resolved to combat and conquer this part of my character before others discovered it and sent me spiraling into a bottomless pit of shame. I learned all I could about fear and faith, prayed hard, asked prayer ministers to intercede for me, held thoughts captive, claimed the promises of God in Scripture, refused to let anxiety dictate my decisions, and hoped that my deep foreboding would dissipate over time. But on the retreat, I saw what I couldn't see in the busyness of everyday life: My determined efforts yielded only minimal progress.

I had finally come to the end of myself. In the bare cinderblock room attached to the humble retreat house, sometime in the middle of the night, I inwardly collapsed and accepted defeat. Powerless to change this embarrassing and tormenting part of my character, I asked Jesus to come into my fear to be with me and help me. He did. Over the succeeding years, we have come far in the freedom that once eluded me. What I needed most was to have Jesus with me, to finally embrace Him and allow Him to live close to me in that lonely place. Holding onto Him there as He held onto me—long before we made progress toward growth—brought so much relief, rest, and hope to my tired soul.

We will talk much more in the chapters ahead about the nuts and bolts of life together with Jesus in a particular room like fear. We'll devote an entire week to identifying the first room we invite Him into. Then, we can outline some things to consider before entering the room and a proposed course of action after opening the door and walking in together. But before we press ahead, I want to take a moment to address a major requirement for this step we're about to take: humility.

We must be humble. I realize that this necessity presents a problem. While it's easy to understand the theoretical importance of meekness in the life of faith, we typically don't know what it looks like on the ground in real life. Strange, huh? I managed to be a devoted church member for decades without a good grasp of humility. I just absorbed the idea put in front of me, and that notion was permeated with pictures of men who were *yielded* and *small*. We often spoke of model congregants who routinely submerged their desires and intentions to give way out of deference to others. These brothers blended in with the background, and those around me praised them for their inconspicuousness. I couldn't help but feel that I would "arrive" in the Christian life only when I finally disappeared. Is this an accurate understanding of humility?

Yes and no. While our fundamental posture before God is yielded and small, we are not called to be smaller than God made us to be and passive in our roles and relationships. Instead, we are to live into our God-given design as Moses did.

Last year, my pastor pointed out that Moses was the humblest man on the entire planet:

> *Now the man Moses was very meek, more than all people who were on the face of the earth.*
>
> Numbers 12:3

Now, that's saying something, especially when we remember that Moses was the leader of an entire nation at this time—approximately a million citizens on the march in the wilderness. He was commander, prophet, and judge over Israel. He was a man God spoke with face to face (Num. 12:8).

So, what made Moses so humble? He was fully in reality with God. He held an accurate view of God and of himself. Therefore, he both felt and acted in ways that were appropriately obedient, respectful, and submissive to his Lord. Moses was no bigger or smaller than he was sovereignly designed to be as he fulfilled his calling to lead God's chosen people. May we also choose to live lives that more closely approximate his life.

Next week will be a little different. It's time for a break. We have laid the groundwork for the weeks ahead, and soon, we will choose a particular hidden chamber of our hearts to open to Jesus. So, let's take a deep breath before we jump—right after giving ourselves to another prayer project.

Prayer Project

1. Take some extended time to review our updated understanding of growth in character trouble spots (Page 38). What about this approach means the most to you? What concerns you? Talk with God about this.

2. How have you understood humility? What has meekness looked like to you?

3. What do you think about the idea that humility means embracing the whole truth? How do you feel about living more fully in reality with Jesus? Liberated and restful? Restricted and anxious?

4. Revisit Question 4 from last week's prayer project—sit quietly with God, meditating on this thought:

   "Apart from You, I can do nothing. Jesus, I need You."

Break

A Time to Rest

I haven't mentioned this before, but my father partnered with me on this writing project. He reads each week's material and gives me his feedback. Last week, he responded, "I think it might be time for a break."

He's probably right. I wouldn't be surprised if many of us feel fatigued this week. It takes a lot of energy to carve out time for a journey like this and look beneath the surface of our lives. We need some time away occasionally to breathe, replenish spent resources, and consolidate our thoughts. So, let's put down this book for the week.

I realize some of you won't have the slightest problem calling a time-out and enjoying this rest stop. I'll bet there are others who would feel more comfortable with something to do. So, I have included a prayer project that might be attractive to you.

Bless you, as you relax and restore. See you next week.

Prayer Project

I have found that time in nature is vital to my spiritual and emotional health. So, why not spend an hour or so in the great outdoors? Try to find a place that feels very spacious and is relatively quiet. Then, pick a comfortable place to sit. Just *be* there for a full sixty minutes. If you'd like, follow these three simple steps:

1. Ask God this sweeping question: "Lord, would you open to me whatever you know is good for me?"
2. Now, just stay quiet and try not to think about anything—release whatever agenda or expectations you might have. Allow your mind to loosen, settle, and clear a bit. You don't want to

search for anything; you just want to be with God and receive whatever He has for you. Maybe He wants you to rest. Maybe He wants to show you something. Let the time be whatever it is.

3. When you return home, take a few minutes to write down what this experience with God was like for you. Then, give Him thanks.

Which Room First?

Welcome back. Did you enjoy the breathing space last week? You were very much on my mind. I have several questions that I wish I could ask you in person over a good cup of coffee: Were you surprised by how tired you felt? Did you manage to carve out some time to replenish? What did you do, and what was the experience like for you? Did anything helpful come to mind during your time away? I realize it takes a lot of mental and emotional strength to intentionally look beneath the surface of our hearts. I hope you could relax, rest, and restore the energy you have spent. Bless you, as we press forward together.

This week, we pivot from the theological foundation-building of Weeks 1 through 5 to the practical steps we must take to live with Jesus in a particular pocket of troublesome character. To assist us in making a smooth turn, I've divided the chapter into three sequential parts. In Part 1, we will identify and name some places in our hearts that we try to keep out of sight. In Part 2, we'll discern which of these hidden rooms tops our list for engagement with Jesus. Finally, in Part 3, we prepare ourselves for the significant step coming up in Week 7: opening the door.

You ready?

Let's jump in.

PART 1—Identifying places in our hearts that we try to keep out of sight

Chances are, you already have a sense of the character challenges that haunt you. Something made you pick up this book. At the same time, we all have blind spots. So, it might be helpful to think back to Week 1 and the many ways God speaks to us about our hidden faults. What do we hear when we listen to our lives with Him?

God speaks directly to us not only through the Word but also via impressions we receive in prayer. He often communicates indirectly as well. For example, what comes up when we listen to sermons, engage in worship, or fellowship with our brothers and sisters in the church body? What's going on at home with our wives and children? What are they telling us? How are we doing on the job? When we go through difficult times, do we notice something? If we listen to our lives, we might discover that God is highlighting something He wants us to know.

This way of hearing from God demands openness. After all, we don't know what He will show us. Maybe we see anger leaking out in relationships, and we realize it's time to move past our attempts to manage our outbursts and enter the " Anger " room with Jesus. Or we might see that we are controlling and must begin to deal relationally with our need to order our lives in particular ways. Then again, we could notice lust, passivity, anxiety, sadness, or lack of love.

The list goes on.

Of course, I've described some gentler ways to become aware of problem areas in our hearts. There are more dramatic ways we can learn about ourselves. Maybe we fail hard, make an enormous mess, or cause terrible pain for ourselves and others. We might run into catastrophic health issues, unraveling finances, relationship breakups, or crushed dreams. We may grow weary of a life-sapping part of our character or loss of meaning in our lives. The possibilities are seemingly endless and extremely difficult.

Peace to you, brother, if you picked up this book in pain. God is with you, and He loves you without reservation. I trust that the rest of our time together will bring you a strong sense of Jesus's compassion, comfort, and hope.

As we move into the prayer project for Part 1, let's try to keep these three points of reference in mind:

1. Don't look too hard for the character flaws you've repressed. Acknowledge and name only the rooms that you can see clearly without straining.

2. Imagine that the doors to these rooms have signs on them. Write down whatever the signs say. If the door to one of these rooms reads, "Insecurity," "Control," "Lust," "Fear," or "Excessive Worry," for example, try to accept your discovery and document it.

3. Be courageous. We conceal things because we don't want them to be true. Acceptance comes with uncomfortable feelings, and who wants to be uncomfortable? However, significant character growth is almost always accompanied by some level of distress.

Once you record the door signs that are pretty easy to see, I encourage you to walk away from this chapter for a day or two. Let your admission land and settle. No need to run from it anymore and no reason to rush toward some kind of resolution. Just spend time with God in reality.

Prayer Project

1. In a quiet place where no one will disturb you, open your heart to God. Ask Him to walk you through your shared home and help you recognize the rooms you have closed off to Him and maybe yourself. Take your time and write down whatever the signs say on the doors to these chambers.

2. Ask the Lord, "How do I feel about these rooms we've identified and documented? How would I complete the sentence, 'If I have these rooms inside me, **then** it means _____.'"

3. Ask the Lord, "God, even though I drew this conclusion in the 'If/Then' statement above, what is the *objective* implication of owning these parts of my heart? What does the presence of these rooms really mean?"

4. Take some time to talk with God about His disposition toward you and toward these parts of your heart. Remember, you belong to Him, and He accepts the whole truth about you—even the parts He intends to change. He loves you.

5. Reflect for a while on the truth that God is with you, and thank Him for His presence and help:

Trust the Lord with all your heart, and do not lean on your understanding. In all your ways acknowledge him, and he will make straight your paths.

Proverbs 3:5–6

PART 2—Discerning which room we will invite Jesus into

As we move into discernment, it might be good to mention the number of rooms we saw in Part 1. Some of us may have seen one or two hidden chambers. Great. Some of us may have seen many. Also great. We are human and, therefore, complex. Most of us have pushed down a host of trouble spots throughout our lives. Although it's natural to feel overwhelmed or confused by our discovery, we are still doing well. There may be a hundred things wrong with us (I'm letting myself off easy here), but God knows the few that if addressed, would make the most significant difference in our lives.

So, we trust. We don't want to pressurize this discernment process—we are not on the hook to ferret out the elusive *next most important thing.* Here again, we must depend on Jesus. Our task is to ask the question, "Which room first?" He will help us land on the answer.

The question we are left with is, "*How* do we discern our choice of rooms with Jesus?" The temptation is to think hard about our options and maybe catalog the pros and cons of each one. But our decision process, in this case, is not a cognitive exercise as much as a listening activity. I like the way Larry Warner puts it:

"*Take some time to sit with your choice, gently turning it over in your heart . . . to help you open to God and to the inner promptings of the Spirit.*"[9]

---

[9] Larry Warner, Discernment, God's Will and Living Jesus: Christian Discernment as a Way of Life (Concord, MA: Barefoot Publishing, 2016) 142.

Larry's description gives us space to breathe. Discernment is—and needs to be—unrushed. Larry says, "Time is a great friend when it comes to discerning and decision-making." I encourage you, then, to take whatever time you need.

If you're like me, though, time is not your biggest stressor. *Getting it right* is. You want to partner with Jesus in the next most important room, right? I have two thoughts that might help vent some of this pressure. First, start your discernment with a question that points toward God's highest priority in Scripture:

You shall love the Lord your God with all your heart and with all your soul and with all your mind. This is the great and first commandment. And a second is like it: you shall love your neighbor as yourself. On these two commandments depend all the Law and the Prophets.

Matthew 22:37-40

Inspired by these verses, our guiding question might be: "What part of my character erodes the quality of my relationships the most?" Based on Matthew 22, our relationships are with ourselves, God, and others. Likewise, the quality of these relationships is determined by our ability to receive and give love. Remember the "receiving" part of relationships, too. It is vitally important, as the apostle John reminds us:

We love because He first loved us.

1 John 4:19

What a pointed reminder. As we progress in the chapters, we will recognize that God's love for us is the wellspring of all we are and everything we do.

The second thought that could relieve some pressure in "getting it right" is that no matter which room you choose, God will lead you where He wants you to go. He doesn't rely on your decision. He knows you and the part of your heart you need to address. He is also well aware of any limitations you might have in trying to land in exactly the right place with Him. Trust Him and stay as open as you can. He won't let you down. He has undoubtedly been gracious to me this way—I routinely find myself in a different place than the one I set out for.

Prayer Project

1. Ask the Lord, "Lord Jesus, which of these rooms should we live in together now? Please be with me as I take plenty of time to gently turn them over in my heart."
2. As you gently turn over these candidate rooms with God, ask Him, "Lord, which of these rooms hinders my ability to receive and to give love?" Continue to gently turn.
3. Ask the Lord, "God, what do I notice? Where do I sense some gravity in my gut?"
4. Ask the Lord, "Where do we seem to be landing, Lord?"
5. Ask the Lord, "How do I feel about living in this particular room with You? Am I relieved? Scared? Frustrated? Worried? Why, Lord?"

PART 3—Preparing to open the door

We're probably not ready yet to open the door to the room we discerned. Our choice likely causes questions and concerns to rise up within us. When we admit to a character problem and are reasonably prepared to do the work required for growth, several considerations can still push hard against us. Here are the four that have been prominent for me:

-   Do I really want this? A more descriptive version of this question would be, "Do I really want to give up control?" Sometimes, we would rather live with the known, no matter how difficult, than launch into unfamiliar territory with another leading the way. What will Jesus do? What will He require of us? What will the experience be like, and how will it affect those around us?

Questions like these are often attended by powerful fears, like the dread I experienced in 2007 when God made it clear that He wanted me to be free of codependent relationships. I longed for freedom, too, of course. I just didn't want to go through the steps to get there. My resistance sprung from a simple fact: if I invited Jesus into this area of my heart, He would eventually want me to tell the truth. I was used to telling these particular friends what I believed they wanted to hear.

From now on, I must communicate my thoughts, feelings, and desires. The idea paralyzed me.

Danger does this. Suppose I believed that agreement with these particular companions secured the approval I craved. In that case, I'd take a considerable risk whenever I didn't mirror their beliefs, feelings, and desires. What if they *disapproved* of me? Now, I'm not talking about the tame notion of dropping a stone into the pool of my life and allowing the ripples to softly wash over my codependent relationships and cleanse them. I was about to drop a bowling ball into a teaspoon of water. That's how it felt, anyway. I was terrified. But God rolled out the more honest version of myself gently. I survived, and my enmeshed relationships either grew healthier or faded away. I see now that all of the outcomes were necessary.

- Will I be able to handle this? Often, troubled places in our hearts come with difficult feelings like confusion, failure, loneliness, guilt, shame, anger, and sadness.[10] Who wants to sign up for this? What if we get overwhelmed or lose our orientation? It's easy to forget that we have instincts to prevent overexposure to disturbing emotions. Once, when I was overseas, for example, I was so exhausted that my defenses went down and allowed a pocket of deep loneliness and sadness to burst into consciousness with no warning at all. I staggered, overwhelmed and unhinged by these shockingly powerful emotions. Within seconds, though, my protective instincts took over and led me to a place with people around. My mind lifted and cleared as I focused on others. Without a problem, I stuffed those feelings back where they came from and continued with my day.

Therefore, It is unlikely that the full measure of feelings in our secret rooms will engulf us. We approach them gradually with Jesus. And if we ever take on too much, we can always back away and ask someone to guide us, like an experienced pastor, evangelical spiritual director, or

---

[10] I learned that troubled places in our hearts generally carry emotions like anger, pain, and sadness in the following course: Dr. John Coe, "Introduction to Christian Spirituality and Prayer" (lecture, Talbot School of Theology, La Mirada, CA, 2008).

Christian therapist. That's what I did. When I got back to the States after my overseas tour, I found a terrific therapist to help me process the brief and unforgettable experience that troubled me there.

- Will God really be with me and help me? Doubts about our relationship with Jesus come to the fore: Does He really love me? Does He care about this issue I'm facing? Can I trust Him with it? If we don't have a track record of life with God in pockets of troublesome character, we can't help but question His disposition toward us in them. We need time and experience to find answers.

- How long will it take? What we're really asking is, how long will I be uncomfortable? We want relief, so naturally, we'll wonder about a timeline for meaningful change. Of course, we can't know when we will experience significant transformation. We can be sure of only two things: that Jesus understands how hard it is for us to live with this uncertainty and that He will be with us.

If you hold one or more of these concerns (or others), discussing them with God is essential. We don't want to ignore them and drag them into the room with us. They could restrict the openness we need for life-changing togetherness with Jesus. So, let's address these questions now in the prayer project below.

Some thoughts about lust

Suppose this chapter left lust at the top of your list for engagement. In that case, I recommend you jump to Appendix 1 before completing this week's prayer project. Many of us struggle with lust. This problem area is uniquely challenging for men and deserves extra space in this book for expanded discussion. I share some thoughts in the appendix that might prove helpful to you.

Prayer Project

Imagine this scene: you pull together a couple of chairs just down the hall from the door to your chosen room and talk quietly with Jesus.

1. Ask the Lord, "Lord, what is going on in my heart right now? What am I feeling about entering this room with you and living together there?"

2. Take some unhurried time—however long you need—to talk to God about these emotions and whatever concerns you might have. Share with Jesus until you sense that you have poured out your heart to Him. He sees you, and He understands all that you are telling Him.

3. Maybe look at the door in silence with Jesus. Know that He is sitting there with you, loving you, and having compassion toward you. He can lead you forward, and He desires to do just that:

Make me to know your ways, O Lord; teach me your paths. Lead me in your truth and teach me, for you are the God of my salvation; for you I wait all the day long.

Psalm 25:4–5

Week 7

Entering Hidden Rooms Within Our Hearts—First Steps

Week 7 marks a divergence in our journey together. From now on, our *experience* will not keep pace with the *content* of the remaining weeks. It must be so. While we require only six more weeks to map out life with Jesus in a character trouble spot, we'll need many months to walk the route and navigate the terrain ahead. This is the nature of significant transitions.

I pulled the trigger on a significant transition three years ago when I moved from Los Angeles to rural Florida. As much as the City of Angels had to offer, I grew bone-tired of the place's congestion, tight spaces, and busyness. I felt cut off from the earth in the endless stretches of asphalt, concrete, and noise. I had to get out. So, after eighteen years in Southern California, I wrapped up my life there as best I could and headed back to my hometown.

I had visited the small town of my youth many times in the forty years since high school graduation, but living here again took some getting used to. I had to sort through necessities like churches, grocery stores, doctors, dentists, and barbers. Of course, I also had to find my new go-to sawmill. I wanted a solid Florida feel to my home, so I planned to make my furniture out of native woods like cypress and cedar. All this to say, it took a good while—probably eighteen months—to feel settled here.

When we begin to live with Jesus in a once-hidden part of our hearts, we'll also need plenty of time to settle in. However, it's helpful to understand what to do when we walk into the room together. I had a checklist when I landed in Florida. Is there such a thing for landing in a problem area with Jesus?

The best answer to this question is "Yes and no." Granted, being completely directionless might not serve us well once we're in the room with Jesus. We'll walk through some priorities in a moment. But life together with God in this newly-opened chamber is not task-oriented. It is relationally oriented. Therefore, the recommendations outlined below help us connect personally with Jesus. We want to be with Him in reality and learn how to depend on Him.

Here we go.

Once you open the door to your chosen room and walk inside with Jesus, imagine that the two of you pull together a couple of oversized, comfortable chairs and position them side by side, facing the room's contents. Then, sink into your chair and take as many deep breaths as you need to, slowly exhaling. You have done it—you've taken a concrete and courageous step to expand your shared home with Jesus. Spend as much time as you like sitting in silence with Him, resting together, and simply occupying the room with one another. It would be hard to overstate the significance of what is happening:

You are no longer alone in this part of your heart.

You are with Jesus now, and He is 100 percent present to you. He fully forgives you, fully accepts you, and thoroughly loves you in this place. You are safe. It doesn't matter yet how deeply you can receive His reassuring embrace. Just allow the truth to be in the room with you.

There will come a time—maybe days or weeks later—when you feel more settled in your shared space and want to move ahead. Four map references will help you take your first steps forward.

- Take your time. Try to accept up front that addressing a problem area with Jesus is a journey rather than something you do in days, weeks, or months. This can be a high hurdle for men. It was for me. I struggled to adopt a long-term growth perspective for many reasons. First among them was this: I possess an aggressive disposition toward forward movement. I've even found myself grading my days against a singular standard: "Did I move ahead in some meaningful way today?" I'm not alone. I can still hear the voice of the US Ambassador I worked for overseas. He was a huge Texas A&M fan and loved to use football-speak in the office. "How can we move the ball forward?" he asked in our meetings, expecting a good answer. I loved it. So, I don't want to beat myself up over a forward-leaning posture. It has its benefits in many contexts. But the need to feel that we've gained ground every day is unhelpful in spiritual growth and character development. We must learn to hold the tension between wanting to make something happen quickly and knowing we can't. There's more to come on this in Week 8.

- Don't rush toward resolution. This isn't a project. While I understand that our souls may ache for relief, shortcuts do not work. Let's slowly look around the room, taking it all in. What do you see? Try not to speak yet. Accept the truth as it appears to you—it is what it is. Allow your heart and mind to land deeply in reality.

- Again, don't rush toward resolution. When words finally come, try to steer away from conversations about "fixing" your character problem. Your principal aim is to experience—to whatever degree you are able—God's love for you right where you are. Sure, He intends to do something about this troublesome part of your heart, but His desire to change you doesn't mean He does not love you. So, start your talk with Him by exploring this question: "What has it been like for you to live with this repressed region of your heart?"

I imagine that life has been difficult. Keeping your distance from buried content probably required a lot of life-sapping vigilance. How did you feel having a secret room that was isolated from the rest of yourself and from others? How hard was it to keep the secret? When did you find yourself controlling people and events to shut down the possibility of exposure? Were there times when something leaked out of the room and into the rest of your life? What happened? Who was affected? What was that like for you? The Lord cares about your life and how you've experienced it. Unburden your heart to Him:

Trust in him at all times, O people; pour out your heart before him; God is a refuge for us.

Psalm 62:8

As you release the contents of this part of your soul to Jesus, try to receive His compassion for you. And try—as best you can—to be compassionate toward yourself.

- Ask Jesus to own this part of your heart and lead you forward. Now that you have more fully accepted your character flaw and its impact on your life, you can better appreciate your need for Jesus. It's time to let go. Tell Jesus that you are willing to submit to Him in utter dependence. Tell Him that you want to learn to rely on His ways and His timing. Your experience with this part of your character over the years is now your ally: you know that you are not going to make anything happen in your own understanding and strength (John 15:5).

Bless you, brother; I know this can be difficult. I hope you experience some relief when you reach the point of submission on this journey. You rely on Jesus's resources now:

Blessed are the poor in spirit, for theirs is the kingdom of heaven.

Matthew 5:3

When we realize—in our depths—that we just can't change on our own, then we live more fully in reality and open our souls to unlimited help from above.

Next week, we'll continue to plot the route ahead of us in our new life with Jesus in this chosen region of our heart. Until then, please work through the prayer project below.

Prayer Project

1. Ask the Lord, "God, what am I thinking and feeling about the slow pace of character change? Am I okay with it? Do I struggle with it? Why, Lord?"

2. Try to make a start now. Open the door to the room you've chosen, walk in with Jesus, and pull together those big chairs. Sink in. Breathe. Sit in silence for a while—however long you like. Rest with Jesus and simply occupy the room with Him. At different times during the week, continue to come together with Him in this place. The remaining map references in this chapter are available to you whenever you choose to take those steps.

3. Slowly read through Psalm 23 a few times:

   The Lord is my shepherd; I shall not want. He makes me lie down in green pastures. He leads me beside still waters. He restores my soul. He leads me in paths of righteousness for his name's sake. Even though I walk through the valley of the shadow of death, I will fear no evil, for you are with me; your rod and your staff, they comfort me. You prepare a table before me in the presence of my enemies; you anoint my head with oil; my cup overflows. Surely goodness and mercy will follow me all the days of my life, and I shall dwell in the house of the Lord forever.

   Psalm 23:1–6

Week 8

Entering Hidden Rooms Within Our Hearts—Next Steps

I n the days leading up to writing this week's chapter, I have carried a single and powerful desire for you: to *know that you are loved*. There is no part of your heart that makes you unlovable. You are chosen:

> *And you also are among those Gentiles who are called to belong to Jesus Christ.*
>
> Romans 1:6 NIV

Nothing can separate you from His love (Rom. 8:35–39). You are His, even if some parts of your character don't belong to Him yet.

We could become uncomfortable, frustrated, or dismissive when love takes center stage in our conversation. Even though God's love for us is a primary change agent in our sanctification journey, it seems easier to comprehend His general love for the world than His individual, unique, and infinite love for each one of us, His sons. Many of the men I talk with long for a deeper knowledge of God's affection, and they struggle to understand why it's not happening in their lives. Others use emphatic tones to communicate the certainty of God's particular love. Their words seem to describe a compelling notion rather than personal experience. Still more focus hard on obedience and choose not to pursue real life experience of this elusive biblical truth. At the end of the day, many of us are left with a troubling question: "If God's love changes me, how do I come to *know* this transforming love more deeply?"

You're doing it.

God could bring a more profound knowledge of His affection for us in any number of ways. But one of the ways that stands out most to me is this: we let Jesus love us in the truth of ourselves. Last week, you took a significant step in this direction when you chose to live together with Jesus in one of your secret rooms. Only through honesty with Him can we know He loves us in the raw reality of who we are. The abstract knowledge of His unconditional disposition toward us becomes more concrete and personal, and we move toward a new way to live in our broken places. *From a resting place of shared life and love,* we submit to Jesus's leadership and receive the help we need in whatever forms and times are best for us.

I hope this perspective encourages you, brother. The path you're on leads to good places. It's time now to walk on with Jesus in your chosen room. The four pointers below will help us move forward whenever we're ready. Again, there is no recommended timeline for progress. We need to discern with Jesus when another step might be right for us.

Be where you are

Years ago, I interviewed an applicant for an open position in our organization. Since this job was critical to our mission and required excellent interpersonal skills, the boss assembled a team of three to meet with our leading candidate. He felt that a group interchange would give us the best chance of discerning a good or bad fit.

He was right—each of us experienced the prospective hire differently. I found connecting with the candidate particularly difficult. We asked questions to better understand his thoughts on various challenging scenarios. His answers seemed highly filtered. I heard what I believed he wanted me to hear. I didn't get to know the man behind the answers. When the interview ended, he left the room. The three of us remained behind and discussed the encounter. I remember my one-sentence assessment: "I feel like we interviewed his representative." Whoever this man was, he didn't show up in the room.

Genuine relationships demand authenticity. When we are in the room with Jesus, we don't want to stay in the background while our "representative" tells Him what we believe He wants to hear. We show up. If we're in a room called "Anger," then it's best to be angry with God. If we are in a "Pain" room, it's best to be in pain with God. We let Him in. If we're anxious, let's be anxious. If we're afraid, be afraid. The only way we can know God's love and concern in the truth of ourselves is to be truthful with Him.

Slowly move into forensics.

At the end of Week 7, we described to Jesus what it's been like for us to live in our secret room, and we asked Him to own this part of our hearts and lead us forward. Where do we go from here? What course might we follow in our ongoing conversation? I suggest you do some good detective work.

The best investigators ask lots of good questions. Their queries help them unpack, examine, and sniff out what happened and why. The same is true with us now. We want to snoop around our secret room with Jesus.

Maybe an example would help. We could pick any character issue to investigate. I've found that anger is an area that needs special attention for many men. So, how would we unpack this part of our hearts?

First, start with whatever might be going on in the present moment. As you explore your anger with Jesus, be angry with Him. If you're mad, you're mad. Maybe you're enraged. Later, as your rage dissipates, describe to Jesus the specific situation that sparked your response. What set you off?

Next, take some time to go beyond what happened and explore what it's like to be angry about the situation you just described. For example, what is happening in your mind? What are you thinking about? How do you feel about being so irritated?

Then you might ask yourself and Jesus a question I first heard from Dr. John Coe: "Is my level of anger proportional to the offense?"[11] In other words, is your response disproportionate to the situation that sparked it? Many of us who struggle with anger can quickly become furious

---

[11] Dr. John Coe, "Introduction to Christian Spirituality and Prayer" (lecture, Talbot School of Theology, La Mirada, CA, 2008).

over occurrences that don't warrant such a strong response. We must take some time to talk with Jesus about this. If we see and accept that our anger is disproportionate to the perceived offense, we are better motivated to proceed with our investigation. We might begin to notice that we are not only triggered more frequently than we would like to be, but our responses are often bigger than objectively reasonable.

At some point, we'll want to know why we are easily set off and why our responses are over the top. It's time for more questions. We might ask something like this: Where is my anger coming from? What is its source? How did it get there? What am I *really* angry about? Is there something in common among the circumstances that spark my anger? What is it? What does this thread tell me about the potential source of my anger? If my rage could speak, what would it say?

We don't know when or how answers to questions like these will come. Maybe Jesus opens a direct answer for us. Or perhaps we identify with someone going through a similar experience and find an answer through his story. It could be a movie, sermon, book, article, song, passage of Scripture, or an off-the-cuff comment we overhear in a coffee shop. As one of my favorite television sleuths says, "The information is out there; you just have to let it in."[12]

Be willing to explore layers.

Top-shelf investigators also go wherever the evidence leads them. Years ago, I asked one of the questions we just talked about: "If my anger could speak, what would it say?" It took a while for the answer to emerge, but it eventually came to me in the form of another question: "What about me?" I realized I felt like my own needs and desires were routinely overridden by people in my life pursuing their own preferences. This common thread ran through so many of my anger episodes. I was on to something—I had another piece of the puzzle that opened the way to more discoveries.

So, let's be prepared to go deeper. Often, the root of our issue runs far

---

12 Jesse Stone: Stone Cold, directed by Robert Harmon (2005; Culver City, CA: Sony Pictures), https://www.amazon.com/Jesse-Stone-Cold-Tom-Selleck/dp/B008YZ4RR0/.

beneath the surface. Wounds and pain spawn all sorts of problematic character challenges, anger included. We had to cope somehow . . . so don't be surprised if the room you enter with Jesus has another door hidden somewhere behind all the clutter. There could be a room behind that door holding more answers. For example, anger may lead to unresolved pain. Control may lead to unresolved insecurity. Fear may lead to a lack of ability to receive love. Just follow the evidence trail with Jesus as best you can.

Here's where an old saying seems to fit: "It gets harder before it gets better." I don't doubt that our search for truth will be more challenging before it lightens. The deeper we go, the stronger the emotions might be. I know that experiencing powerful feelings can be troubling. At the same time, you probably don't have to look far to see the consequences of choosing not to. I've known many men—some in weighty church and parachurch leadership positions—who struggled with terrible anger, for example. More than a few of these leaders were well into their sixties. Unfortunately, they had not wholly entered into reality with God. In their room called "Anger," they saw another door leading to the deeper pain that fueled their aggression. In some cases, they knew what was in that next room—the people and events that had deeply wounded them. And they had no trouble talking in generalities about these experiences. However, no sorrow made its way into their story. Simply put, these men did not enter that room with Jesus— they kept their distance from it and did not bring their profound hurt into their relationship with Him. I wonder how much of their lives was subverted and how much damage was done while gripped in the clutches of anger for six decades. Heartbreaking.

Be open to various forms of help.

As we follow where the evidence leads, there may be times when we need some extra help. I did. I still do. My mantra before diving into hidden rooms with Jesus was catchy and convincing: "I'm with Jesus— we've got this." He and I could take on anything together. And who could argue with that, right? Who would be willing to challenge the view that Jesus is enough?

I was a slow learner in matters of the heart, but what I did learn stuck. The Bible does not prescribe a solo journey with God toward greater maturity. Scripture elevates community and mutual dependence. We have many needs, and God often uses people to supply what we lack. So, if we are in one of our hidden rooms with Jesus and find that we lack perspective, discernment, direction, human companionship, trust, strength, hope, or anything else, let's be humble and courageous enough to ask someone to walk with us for a while.

God can rally resources and people to meet these unfolding needs. Maybe your pastor has been on a journey like yours and can connect with you regularly. Perhaps a group of like-minded men has space for you to join them. You might also find sharing your experience with a spiritual director, Christian therapist, or seasoned prayer minister helpful. All of these people are there to support you.

It might be challenging to embrace some forms of help at first. Spiritual direction and therapy, in particular, could be areas of concern for us. Maybe we don't know anything about spiritual direction, and psychology may sound suspicious to some. I include some helpful information about spiritual direction in Appendix 2. I'll take a moment now to talk about therapy.

I started therapy many years ago when part of my life collapsed, and I was having a terrible time finding my way out of the rubble. I was forced into it. Until that time, I believed several things about therapeutic help:

- Seeing a psychologist was evidence of a lack of faith. If I truly believed, the Holy Spirit and the Scriptures were sufficient for my needs. As I mentioned earlier, I was sure that Jesus and I should be able to take on anything together. We didn't require outside assistance.

- Psychology was a crutch for the weak. Of course, I had no intention of appearing weak. I was too insecure to risk the loss of my well-crafted image. I believed others saw me as a strong man, and I planned to keep it that way.

- Psychotherapy is dangerous. A therapist could steer me off course or cause me to lose my way altogether.

Obviously, I was a hard sell. But there's nothing like a personal crisis to get us past uninformed views like the ones I held and force us to reach out for a hand up.

As it turns out, therapy has been one of God's greatest kindnesses to me. Of course, I didn't sign on with just anybody. I got referrals from trusted people and met only with devout Christian therapists who saw their work as a calling to ministry. I took time to discern and develop trust as well. My experience with these unique, gifted people was earth-shaking.

We've already covered a lot of ground this week, so I'll get right to the point: my therapists helped me open my soul to God in profoundly deeper ways. These expert guides and supportive companions enabled me to live with Jesus—day by day—in previously unapproachable corridors and rooms in our shared home. This experience was not untethered; my appetite for the Word only grew as Jesus and I spent time exploring together. His truth and love drew me forward and closer, and I expanded into a more robust masculinity. So, if the time comes when you want to reach out for this kind of support, go for it. Just check in with your pastor—most churches have referral lists with contact information for therapists they trust.

Next week, we'll discuss more pointers to help us stay grounded as we live and grow with Jesus in our chosen room. Until then, I hope you take as much time as necessary to digest this week's content and engage with the prayer project. Peace to you, brother.

Prayer Project

1. What do you think about God's love for you being a primary change agent in your sanctification journey? Do you buy in? Not so much? What questions do you have? Take some time to talk with God about those questions.

2. When you think about being wherever you are with Jesus and allowing the emotions in your secret room to be out in the open, are you comfortable? Uncomfortable? Why? What needs to happen for you to grow more comfortable?

3. What part of this week's content brought you hope? Why? Maybe spend some time thanking God for this.

4. What part of this week's content do you feel uncomfortable with? Why? Try to talk with Jesus about this. What might you need from Him to move forward?

Entering Hidden Rooms Within Our Hearts—Settling In (Part 1)

Now that we are underway with Jesus in a once-repressed part of our hearts, it's a good time to discuss the future. How do we stay in the growth process with Him over the following months and years? This question is more about perspective and posture than tasks. We've already discussed the pace of change—that we want to be unrushed in our expanded living space with Jesus. What else do we need to remember as we move forward? I've found four pointers particularly helpful:

- Keep the essentials in front of us.
- Adjust our aimpoint.
- Understand the place of emotions.
- Make space for whatever work Jesus requires of us.

We'll look at the first two pointers in this chapter and pick up the last two in Week 10.

Keep the essentials at the forefront.

Some choices we make change our lives forever. For example, when we ask Jesus to save us, we become Christians for all eternity. If we marry, we are husbands for the rest of our lives. Having children makes us fathers and potentially grandfathers. Likewise, we experience a dramatic and permanent change when we bring a hidden character issue into our shared living space with Jesus: *we are no longer alone.* We are with

Him now—this is the most fundamental change we could make, and it is impossible to overstate its importance. Also, among countless other things, He brings two more essential truths to our journey: *He loves us*, and *He is in control*.

Let's take a brief look at these three crucial changes:

- We are no longer alone. One word comes to mind when I think about Jesus entering a room: impact. Without a doubt, we know that His presence influences everything around Him. That's why we're reluctant to acknowledge Him when we intend to do something we shouldn't do. The first action we must take to engage in sin is to push Jesus out of our minds and imagine that He isn't there, right? This understanding of Jesus's impact in a room becomes our ally and a rich source of hope. We know with certainty that change is coming. We *will* see movement. Of course, Jesus isn't some impersonal force; progress is relationally oriented. He is the One who created us, loves us, and shows us compassion without restraint. He maintains a steadfast commitment to our growth (Rom. 8:29).

- We are loved in reality. When do we feel most loved? Is it when we're at our best or at our worst? I used to believe I had to be close to perfect to be loved. This belief is not uncommon. Many of us feel more loved when we're put together and doing everything well. However, I found that my attempts to be good all the time brought mixed results. On one hand, I felt affirmed when others paid attention to the parts of my character they valued. These people strengthened me and encouraged me to further develop the traits they appreciated and respected. On the other hand, I felt like I had to keep my weaknesses hidden to hold onto their love, and life became lonely and exhausting.

When I finally dared to share some of my deficiencies with others, I discovered a more transformative way to live. The closest people in my life still loved me despite my flaws. In fact, we grew closer to one another through more authentic and vulnerable connections. The same holds true with Jesus. Over time, He demonstrates a steadfast love that does not diminish when we open our secret rooms to Him. His unconditional care becomes much more real to us in our weak and broken places. We are getting closer to the essence of growth: receiving God's love for us more deeply.

- We are not in control. Dependence on Jesus brings freedom, hope, and rest. We are no longer on the hook to figure out what's going on in our pocket of troublesome character and devise a strategy to fix or at least manage it. Jesus leads now. While we often feel powerless to understand and to change this part of our hearts, He holds the answers and the way forward. We can breathe. We can lean into Jesus and let the burden of solo responsibility for growth slide off our shoulders and onto the ground. It's time to learn how to be at rest in Him and to trust Him with our desire for change.

We simply want to hold onto these three essentials because we tend to forget them. When the work required for growth gets tough, and change comes slowly, it's easy to become frustrated and look for a quicker path to relief. I don't think we should beat ourselves up when this happens. We all forget important things occasionally, and God is not surprised when we do. He knows we're prone to lose perspective. He uses the word "remember" or one of its variants several hundred times in the Scriptures. It would be time well spent to sit in the room with Jesus once in a while to think about these three truths with Him and enjoy the relief and rest they bring to our souls.

Adjust our Aimpoint

Our destination is a process.

I'm not trying to bend our minds with this statement or let us off the hook for substantive change. The truth is, we are always on the way. We are constantly becoming more fully the men God created us to be in our problem areas.

In the Western world, we like toggle-switch thinking, don't we? The switch is either on or off—mysteries are solved, problems are fixed, goals achieved, and missions accomplished. We absorb this mindset from our culture, communities, and families. Almost every aspect of our education and training reinforces the paradigm as well. No doubt, this perspective permeated my military career. The most respected men and women in the Air Force carried reputations as fixers. They knew how to throw the switch.

When we grow with Jesus in a pocket of troublesome character, though, we do not fix something; we *become* something. What we become is not only for our own sake but also for the sake of others. For example, if I struggle with insecurity, I want to be freer and less insecure over time. But my larger objective is to love well, no longer hindered by my secret fears. If worry is my issue, I not only want to be more trusting, settled, and at peace. I desire to love others with more of myself present to them rather than sidelined with anxiety. In all of our character challenges, our primary aim is to love robustly and well.

At the same time, we don't know the path we'll take to get there. Once we're in a secret room with Jesus, we understand how we might begin with Him. Weeks 8 and 9 mapped out some first steps. Beyond these initial steps, though, the path to personal freedom and mature love is hidden in this part of our hearts. The way ahead holds unforeseeable occurrences that will emerge in unexpected ways at unpredictable times. We cannot anticipate what will happen on this journey with Jesus or how long it will take. Only He knows what is uniquely best for us.

Therefore, it is reasonable to embrace *engagement* or *process* as our destination. We just want to be where we need to be—in the room with Jesus and in the process of becoming. Suppose we can switch from one set of gears in the room (task and timeline) to a completely different set (relationship and process). In that case, we can posture ourselves for the journey to come. Try to be patient and kind with yourself. Changing gears is not easy, nor is it quick.

A process-oriented approach to growth brings many benefits. Four come to mind:

- A *process orientation* facilitates dependence and trust. When Jesus is the center of our attention, we experience raw reliance on Him. Reliance brings freedom. We slowly shed the impossible burden we shouldered, believing that growth was all on us. Correspondingly, our trust rises over time as we see Him work to bring us whatever we need to develop the character we long for.

- A *process orientation* focuses our efforts. Since the path of growth is obscure, we can only do what is right in front of us. If He has us simply sitting in the room with Him, then that's what we give ourselves to. Suppose He connects us with a helpful resource, like a book, article, podcast, sermon, passage of Scripture, song, movie, or anything else. In that case, we explore and process the resource with Him. We live in the present moment as best we can, knowing that future moments –and our preparedness for them—are in His hands.

- A *process orientation* depressurizes the journey. We're not in charge. We'll talk more next week about personal effort in this process of becoming. Hard work is certainly required at times. But we are not in charge—we are yoked to Jesus now:

Take my yoke upon you, and learn from me, for I am gentle and lowly in heart, and you will find rest for your souls. For my yoke is easy, and my burden is light.
Matthew 11:29–30

Jesus pulls much of the load, and He guides us down the path that's best for us:

Let me hear in the morning of your steadfast love, for in you I trust. Make me know the way I should go, for to you I lift up my soul.
Psalm 143:8

When we are in the room with Jesus, open to Him and willing to follow however He leads, we can finally say that we are doing all we can do.

- A *process orientation* builds the bond we ache for. We will find that the more we expand our home with Jesus, the more we realize He is our deepest need and core desire. With more of His presence in our character trouble spots, we will grow more comfortable and content simply being on the way together. We'll be satisfied with real life—the process of always becoming more fully the men He made us to be.

Next week, we'll pick up the last two of our four-pointers for sustaining good perspective and posture in the room with Jesus. For now, let's work through this week's prayer project.

Prayer Project

1. Find some unhurried time in a quiet place to sit with God and let your soul unwind. Ponder the three essential truths in the room with Jesus: you are not alone anymore; you are loved in the truth of yourself; and you are no longer in control. What reactions do you notice? Do you feel unburdened? Worried? Talk with Him about this.

2. When you frame the growth process as the "destination," are you on board? Are you relieved? Frustrated? Take some time to discuss your disposition with Jesus.

3. Ask God and ask yourself, "Lord, where am I with the idea that my true objective in this room with you is not only relief but a greater ability to love well? How does this sit with me? What do I like about this goal? What do I not like?"

4. Revisit Proverbs 3:5-6, slowly reading through these verses several times:

   Trust in the Lord with all your heart, and do not lean on your own understanding. In all your ways, acknowledge him, and he will make straight your paths.

   Proverbs 3:5–6

Entering Hidden Rooms Within Our Hearts—Settling In (Part 2)

Last week, we discussed the first two of four helpful pointers for our ongoing growth process in a once-repressed part of our hearts. This week, we'll talk about the last two: understanding the place of emotions and making space for whatever work is required of us. I saved these two for last because they might be more challenging to embrace. As I consider my experience in secret rooms with Jesus—past and present—I notice that I push back on these two points of growth.

Understand the place of emotions in the room

We must allow ourselves to feel emotions in the room.

It might be good to stop for a moment and take notice of your reaction to this statement. Does guidance like this make you suspicious, disappointed, or frustrated? It's not uncommon to be wary of our emotions. Many of us learned long ago that we can't trust our feelings. We routinely find our emotions pulling us in directions that aren't good for us, don't we? And haven't we heard story after story of men who allowed their feelings to lead them down destructive paths? Paths that left them sideways with Scripture and those closest to them?

No doubt, we have cause for caution. We must take a mature view. While it is potentially dangerous to blindly follow our feelings, it is also hazardous to repress them. Ongoing suppression is an overreaction to the perceived threat of emotional influence. Suppression is an unhealthy safeguard that only creates more problems for us. I get that we don't want to feel some of these uncomfortable feelings. Locking them in a closet at the back of the room is attractive, especially if this simple action protects us from skidding into sinful thoughts, attitudes, and behaviors. However, we don't want our emotions *or fears* to lead the way without our minds engaged. We must choose to *deal with our feelings* rather than thoughtlessly obey them or fearfully bury them. Because here's the thing: You've got to feel it to heal it.

I first heard these words when a small group of friends and I went to a workshop on God's healing presence. I don't remember the speaker's name who dropped this pithy phrase. I remember only two things about him: One, he had a well-respected prayer ministry, and two, he casually moved on after burping up these eight words without unpacking them at all. My mind exploded. "What?! Is this the best you can do?" I thought. "I'm an engineer—you don't care to offer a systematic, rigorous, and comprehensive defense for such a 'squishy' pronouncement?" I understood what the man was saying, but my inability to validate his claim frustrated me. I could not stay with him as he moved on with the rest of his talk. I just sat there with my brain locked.

Almost a year would pass before I could receive his statement and begin to put it into my own words. What he was saying was this: we have to *be in reality with God* to find deep healing and growth. We can't sit with Jesus in the room and only talk about the emotions in that closet. Yes, it might be good for us to start there. But if we don't move on to experience these feelings, we can only go so far. At some point, we have to feel our own emotions with Jesus to be fully in reality with Him. We want to be altogether present to each other, right? If you are in a room called "Anger," and you want to shout the house down, go ahead and roar. If you are in a room called "Pain," and your hurt begins to surface, allow Jesus to be with you in your sorrow. Let the tears flow. If you are worried, then worry with Him. Pace the floor and rattle on about all the what-ifs that haunt you. Don't hold back.

Keep in mind, too, that emotions in the room usually come and go. Sometimes we'll feel them, and sometimes we won't. Our task is not to experience our emotions every time we're in this part of our house with

Jesus but to integrate the room into our shared living space. We want to freely go in and out of this once-hidden place in our hearts. No need to stay longer than necessary at any one time.[13] In the beginning, spend reasonable chunks of time there. Don't get overwhelmed. You just need enough space to press into the work that Jesus opens before you, bit by bit, whether He leads you to feel your emotions or to do something very different. And, speaking of work, we'll likely have plenty to do.

Make space for necessary work.

A good friend of mine likes to say, "If it were easy, everybody would be doing it." True. Our lives are often full, leaving us little time and energy for the work required to address a character issue deeply. We have obligations at every turn—on the job, at home, and in our churches and communities. Many of us regularly feel the weight of these responsibilities, too. In 2022, the American Institute of Stress reported that seventy-seven percent of Americans experience a level of stress in their lives that affects their physical health, while seventy-three percent have mental health impacts.[14] This is roughly one-quarter of a billion people! If we're under significant stress, we are not alone.

These numbers, my own experiences, and the many conversations I've had with other men tell me that we'll need intentionality and decisiveness to make space to be with Jesus in a character flaw. We might have to adjust some priorities for a season and restructure parts of our routines. After all, if God connects us to resources, like books, sermons, lectures, or tailored Scripture studies, we'll need space to engage with them. Other forms of help He could bring require even more time and, possibly, financial resources. Maybe Jesus leads us to join a group, enroll in a class, or meet regularly with a counselor, spiritual director, or prayer team. Who knows what forms of help He might open to us? But don't worry—He will not overload you.

Jesus knows you and understands your life. He will help you discern

---

[13] Dr. Betsy Barber, "Intensive Journey Inward and Retreat" (lecture, Talbot School of Theology, La Mirada, CA, 2011).

[14] Lacey Skwortz, "Stress Awareness Month," Valley Professionals Community Health Center, accessed November 15, 2023, https://valleyprohealth.org/stress-awareness-month.

the choices that enable you to fulfill your responsibilities while giving reasonable time and attention to your character challenge. Remember that your decisions must also consider the balance you need for physical and mental health. Typically, Jesus does not want you to overwhelm parts of your life while other essential areas languish. He is concerned about you as a whole man.

You will likely find that much of the work required in the room with Jesus is not additive but flows naturally with your life. Once, when Jesus and I were working on the anxiety I experienced in relationships, He led me to make a simple change in my behavior. I used to worry that if somebody had an issue with me, they would back away from our relationship. To lower my anxiety, I would pick up the phone to say hello and to see how they were doing. My objective, of course, was to see how they were doing with me. If, during our talk, I perceived that we were fine, my anxiety dissipated, and I felt better for a while. This form of anxiety management was a regular part of my life, and I gave it little thought.

Jesus showed me what I was doing—these phone calls were about me and my fears. I sensed that He wanted me to stop the check-ins. I had to choose to trust the people in my life and learn to treat them as adults. If they had issues with me, they would approach me about them, right? I agreed to stop the calls.

Of course, when I got anxious again in a relationship, Jesus did not permit me to grab the phone and make these uncomfortable feelings go away. Instead, I sensed He wanted me to be with Him in my uneasiness, unpack it with Him, and follow where it led. So, we did the investigative work and eventually found our way to another room in our shared home. I am happy to say that I trust the people in my life much more now, and I'm much more accessible to them.

Undoubtedly, Jesus can use the most ordinary parts of our everyday lives to move us forward in extraordinary ways. Remember that everything happening in and around the room is useful to Jesus. If we reprioritize or restructure something to engage with a resource He brings, we'll likely bump into an internal reaction. We tend to resist changes like this. It's all part of the journey—share your resistance with

Him. Explore it together. Who knows where it might lead?

Next week, we will tackle the question that almost always arises when discussing growth in a pocket of problematic character: "How far will we go?" Until then, let's meet with God over this week's content.

Prayer Project

1. Ask God and ask yourself, "How do I feel about experiencing my emotions in the room? Am I okay with it? Am I not okay? Why, Lord? How do you want me to think about this?"

2. Re-read the section about making space for whatever work Jesus requires of us in the room. Where does your mind go? Do you feel comfortable with potential adjustments to priorities, schedules, or activities? Is the possibility straining? Why?

3. Write down whatever uncertainties or questions you carry forward from this chapter. Then, take some time to talk them over with God. Ask Him to steer you toward some reasonable resolution to move forward.

4. Spend a few moments meditating on this psalm:

    O Lord, you have searched me and known me! You know when I sit down and when I rise up, you discern my thoughts from afar. You search out my path and my lying down and are acquainted with all my ways. Even before a word is on my tongue, behold, O Lord, you know it altogether. You hem me in, behind and before, and lay your hand upon me. Such knowledge is too wonderful for me; it is high; I cannot attain it.

    Psalm 139:1–6

How Far Will We Go?

When I was a boy, my parents said that time goes by faster as we get older. Back then, I thought, "Yeah, whatever." Now I think, "Wow, they were right." It's hard to believe we have only two weeks left in our journey together. So, let's carve out space this week to address a question that may have been growing in the back of our minds: What's the payoff? How far will we go if we put forth the effort to change a challenging part of our character?

I would like to say, "All the way." Wouldn't it be great if there were no trace of anger in our hearts after Jesus and we spent enough time together in that room (and in the rooms adjoining it)? Or no remnants of worry? God could make this happen, of course. He could transform our doubt into complete trust and our anxiety into perfect peace. He could take our ravenous greed and reshape it into unfettered generosity. However, it must be a rare exception to experience 100 percent change in a troublesome part of our hearts. God seems to reserve perfection for heaven; He doesn't take us from total depravity to a spotless life while we are still in the world.

So, again, how far *will* we go? The best answer to this question is "far enough." And far enough is *dramatic*.

Let's conduct a thought experiment to help us understand this answer. Imagine a marble resting at the bottom of a large wooden bowl. Our marble is half an inch in diameter, and the bowl is, say, nine inches across at the top and four inches deep. Now picture this: you reach inside the bowl and flick the marble with your index finger. What happens?

When I flick the marble in my mind, it rockets up the side of the bowl like it won't stop. Gravity wins, though, and the little sphere reverses its course, races down the bowl, and shoots up the other side. Up and down—round and round—it flies about the container, looking agitated. Meanwhile, the pull of gravity patiently overcomes the energy I put into the glass ball when I sent it on its course. After a little more time, nature's persistent force prevails, and my marble rolls toward its resting place. With a slight wobble, as if to get in the last word, it stops at the bottom of the bowl.

Now, imagine that you retrieve the exhausted marble and replace it with another three times its size. Repeat the experiment, flicking your new subject with approximately the same force as the first. Yeah, this is going to hurt your finger. But smack it anyway. What do you see?

Not much. When I flick my boulder, it heads toward the side of the bowl without much enthusiasm. It rides up the side only a little, then rolls down through the bottom and touches the other side as if obligated. In no time, the bigger glass ball rests at the bottom like nothing happened.

But the same thing *did* happen to both marbles. We placed each one in the same position in the same bowl. We flicked them both with roughly the same force. The first took off like it would break containment and fly out of the bowl. The second lumbered a bit at the bottom, then quickly came to rest. It makes sense that if we want to agitate both masses to the same degree, we must impart a lot more energy to the second marble-and-bowl system than we did to the first.

So it is with our pockets of troubled character. As we mature with Jesus in a once-hidden room, we may not see our character challenge completely disappear. But we will see the problem diminish as Jesus re-forms that part of our hearts, radically changing its effect on our lives.[15] We'll grow healthier, bigger, stronger, steadier, and more settled. We won't be so easily overtaken by our weaknesses anymore. Look at worry, for example. After abiding with Jesus in this room for years now, I am still prone to worry. However, it takes a lot more disruption in

---

[15] Dr. Judy TenElshof, "Spiritual Disciplines Seminar" (lecture, Talbot School of Theology, La Mirada, CA, 2011).

my life to trigger my anxiety. Just as important, I don't agonize over the disturbance as intensely or for as long as I did before Jesus and I entered that room together. My life is dramatically different—trust and freedom have much more sway in my day-to-day experience than fear and worry. This shift is a game-changer, making my life more enjoyable and much less burdensome.

Our Christian lives are a mixed bag of perfection and approximation. When we look at our lives through the lens of perfection, we remember that God has made us perfectly righteous. From the moment we receive the Lord Jesus into our hearts, He credits us with His own righteousness:

> *Indeed, I count everything as loss because of the surpassing worth of knowing Christ Jesus my Lord. For his sake I have suffered the loss of all things and count them as rubbish, in order that I may gain Christ and be found in him, not having a righteousness of my own that comes from the law, but that which comes through faith in Christ, the righteousness from God that depends on faith.*
>
> Philippians 3:8–9

Paul's words tell us that we occupy a fixed position of righteousness—in Christ, by faith. What a grace.

When we switch lenses and look at our lives as approximations, we recognize that our time on earth is largely about the work of sanctification. God intends for our character to grow in pursuit of our positional standing. He calls us into partnership with Him as He works to make us more like Jesus in our uniqueness. This means there is much to be gained in closer and closer approximations of Jesus's character. Even small increases in love, joy, peace, patience, kindness, goodness, faithfulness, gentleness, and self-control can translate to radical changes in our lives, relationships, and witness. Again, what a grace.

I wonder if you feel relieved after reading these first four pages. We don't have to arrive in any particular area of our hearts to experience so much more life—to be bigger, deeper, more consolidated, and sturdier men who are reasonably at peace and loving well. We just have to become *closer approximations* to God's unique design for us. Let's look at one more example since it is common among many of us: anger. While we might not find complete healing of the pain that fuels our anger, chances are that our healing will be substantive. The impact of this partial or approximate healing on our lives and relationships can be dramatic. We may still get angry sometimes, but it will take much greater offenses to trigger our aggressive responses. And whatever retorts we do let fly will not be as raw and unfiltered as they once were. We will feel more at ease and free. No doubt, those around us will, too.

We have a lot to look forward to. However, we've talked only about the distance we might travel in the room we entered with Jesus in Week 7. There's more. When we travel far in this particular part of our character, we also mature in other related ways that profoundly impact our lives. Let's look at four of these "connected" ways we grow into more robustly loving men:

- We get to know Jesus better. One of the ways we grow in a relationship with someone is by doing new things together. Whenever we enter an interior room with Jesus, we do just that. We have not been together in this room before. We have not yet partnered to work toward growth in this particular character challenge. We will undoubtedly learn something new about Jesus here, perhaps something in the Word that we haven't closely noticed before. We'll likely deepen what we do know about Him as well, chiefly this:

… What is the breadth and length and height and depth, and to know the love of Christ

Ephesians 3:18–19

When we know more of Jesus's love for us—especially in our broken places—we love Him back more (1 John 4:19). We also love what He loves more. This developing mutual love is the center of our ongoing life together.

- We settle into greater dependence and humility. One of the supreme virtues in our lives with God must be humility. And one of the surest ways to become a humbler man is to experience our raw need for Him. In a once-secret room, it is easier to experience our neediness. We don't know much at all, right? We don't have answers to basic questions like "What do I need to grow?" We have Jesus, and we will learn that He is enough. We can trust Him. We can wait for Him to light up enough of our path to take the next step, then the next. Eventually, we will embrace dependence and humility as a reliable path to personal freedom and spiritual authority.

- We develop a more profound, more powerful ability to help others. We cannot walk alongside others and guide them through rugged terrain—with genuine understanding and compassion— unless we have fruitfully traveled rough ground before. God often uses our own struggles to train us for service to His other sons and daughters and those whom He intends to call to Himself. In Paul's words:

> *Blessed be the God and Father of our Lord Jesus Christ, the Father of mercies and God of all comfort, who comforts us in all our affliction, so that we may be able to comfort Those who are in any affliction, with the comfort with which we ourselves are comforted by God.*
>
> 2 Corinthians 1:3–4

When we open the door to some repressed part of our hearts, we do it for ourselves. But we also do it for others.

- We minister to those around us in healthier ways. One of my most significant weaknesses in ministry has been my secret desire to be needed and singularly helpful. More honestly, I would say that I have longed to be indispensable and invaluable. For a couple of decades, serving others was more about my needs than those I tried to help. I still have some of this tendency to put myself at the center of ministry rather than God. But there's good news: as we go on with God in our hidden rooms, He slowly becomes the center of all. We develop a longing for others to have Him in His fullness, and we find ourselves wincing more often at the thought of getting ourselves mixed up in His activity in another's life. Our desire for recognition and praise slowly shifts. We want more praise to flow to Jesus. We discover that our primary desire is to partner with God—to step in and help a person in need open to Him and cooperate with Him. Then, we must carefully back away, leaving no residue of our involvement. It is enough for us to point to Jesus. Surely, God liberates us from many restraints as we honor Him more than we celebrate ourselves or our image and reputation.

Bless you, brother, as you think on these things.

As we highlighted at the beginning of this chapter, next week will be our last together. So, I'd like to talk about something that I hope will further depressurize our journeys with Jesus and posture us well to restfully follow Him in the future. Until then, of course, we have some work to do in prayer. Peace to you as you open to God.

Prayer Project

1. Ask the Lord, "God, what do I think of the marble in the bowl metaphor? Am I okay with the prospect of substantive change rather than perfect healing and growth? Am I not okay? Why, Lord?"

2. Ask the Lord, "When I sit with the idea of approximating Jesus's character, what reaction do I notice inside? Do I feel relieved? Am I pushing back? Why, Lord?"

3. Ask the Lord, "God, when I look through the four additional ways I might mature in this room with you, what encourages me most? What concerns me most? Why?"

4. Ask the Lord, "How do I feel about the nature of growth? Am I comfortable with our maturation process being relationally based? Am I okay with the timeline looking longer than what I may have hoped for?"

5. Read through or sing these verses several times. The lines are taken from the famous hymn that put Lamentations 3:22-23 to music. Just exhale and rest in God's presence.

> *The steadfast love of the Lord never ceases;*
> *His mercies never come to an end;*
> *They are new every morning;*

New every morning;
Great is thy faithfulness, O Lord;
Great is thy faithfulness.[16]

Now close your time in prayer with this verse:

"The Lord is my portion," says my soul, "therefore I will hope in him."

—Lamentations 3:24

---

16 Edith McNeill, "The Steadfast Love of the Lord," The Hymnary, accessed November 14, 2023, https://hymnary.org/text/the_steadfast_love_of_the_lord_never_mcn.

Week 12

The Journey Never Ends

M y friend Mark and I served together in the military. After we met at a local church gathering, we connected often to share our lives and to process the issues we faced in our assignments and careers. We both placed a high value on decisiveness and aggressive forward movement. Pressing into whatever was before us was central to our developing leadership styles. So, over the years, we generated a few slogans to spur one another on, especially when difficulties pressed hard against us and made progress in our duties painful. My favorite was, "Git' er done!"

I know—where's the compassion, right? But I always knew that behind his words, Mark understood what I was going through. Now, even when I need to fix the flapper valve in my toilet or split some firewood, I hear his voice: "Git' er done!" And not just in my head but in person. We are still as close as brothers.

This aggressive mentality served us well in Air Force life. I also brought this mindset into my Christian life. Many of us do. We can't help it—we've marinated in our culture's task orientation for decades, so we don't always recognize the disposition or the dangers it poses. For example, we might reduce our spiritual exercises, like Scripture reading, prayer, or service, to checklist items that contribute to a good cause. Or we could find ourselves tackling hidden character challenges like a series of self-improvement projects (on reasonable timelines) while pushing Jesus to the margins.

Have you noticed how many professional and spiritual resources, like books, videos, conferences, and workshops, make similar claims? They often promise significant improvements in a short span of time while minimizing personal effort. For example, we might find success if we practice seven proven principles. Or, we can become better managers by studying ten minutes daily, or revamp our ministries in twelve quick steps. We can even grow as disciples in five minutes per day. These resources are helpful—I'm glad that people did the work to sift through an overwhelming number of possibilities for focusing our efforts or building good habits. However, these forms of help seem to have something in common: they are rooted in a task mentality and designed to quickly enhance our *capabilities*.

Sure, there's a place for developing our capabilities, yet I am gut-punched as I sit with this observation. What the world needs most is not more capable men. Knowledgeable men who can make things happen are everywhere. What the world longs for is men who are *different*.

Our families, churches, and communities hunger for men with expansive souls who carry robust love and spiritual authority. Depth, substance, and power, however, are not personal capabilities. Raw influence is not so much about what we say or what we can do. It's about *who we are*. And we become more fully the men God created us to be as we enlarge our interior living space with Jesus and abide with Him. This is the life of true adventure. This is a journey that never ends.

There's always something new to invite Jesus into, isn't there? Maybe after we travel far enough in the hidden room we identified earlier, we open another pocket of character that needs attention. I repressed so much over the years that I had plenty of chambers to integrate into my shared living space with Jesus. I still do. Some of these rooms can even be fun to explore together. God and I are working to enlarge my ability to live in the moment and enjoy myself. What a gift to get out of my head and into my days.

Also, circumstances change occasionally, providing opportunities to walk new ground with Jesus. Seasons come and go as well:

> *For everything there is a season, and a time for every matter under heaven: a time to be born, and a time to die; a time to plant, and a time to pluck up what is planted; a time to kill, and a time to heal;*

*a time to break down, and a time to build up; a time to weep, and a
time to laugh; a time to mourn, and a time to dance; a time to cast
away stones, and a time to gather stones together; a time to embrace,
and a time to refrain from embracing; a time to seek, and a time to
lose; a time to keep, and a time to cast away; a time to tear, and a
time to sew; a time to keep silent, and a time to speak; a time to love,
and a time to hate; a time for war, and a time for peace.*

Ecclesiastes 3:1-8

Changing seasons often expose parts of our hearts that need Jesus.
I'm starting to see that simply getting older reveals places inside that
hold serious questions about meaning, purpose, and a life well-lived.
Someday, Jesus and I will need to spend more time there.

Fortunately, we do not walk this path toward greater spiritual maturity
alone, and we are not without examples to follow. Scripture gives us
glimpses of men who walked with the power we desperately need today,
and we can find strength in their stories. A couple of my favorites are
Peter and John. Remember when God used these men to heal the
disabled man at the entrance to the temple in Jerusalem? Luke tells us
in Acts 4 that Peter preached repentance to the astonished crowd that
evening, and God rescued 5,000 souls.

However, the next day, Peter and John stood before the Sanhedrin, the
Jewish Council that oversaw religious and political life in Israel.[17] The
seventy-one members of the Council asked the two men about the
man they healed: "By what power or by what name did you do this?"
(Acts 4:7). Peter seized the opportunity to launch into a short and
direct explanation that turned the Sanhedrin on its head.

In so many words, Peter told these six dozen men that they had rejected,
tortured, and murdered the long-awaited Messiah, whom God raised
from the dead. Wow—what an accusation! But it's important to note
Peter's disposition—the text gives no indication that he was angry or
judgmental. Instead, he appeared to address the Council respectfully
and say these things to its members matter-of-factly.

---

17 "Sanhedrin," The Holman Illustrated Bible Dictionary (Nashville, TN:
Holman Bible Publishers, 2003), 1445–1446.

Let this sink in for a moment. Peter just calmly dropped an enormous bomb in the crowd. You would expect to see debris flying everywhere and a united, swift, and severe reaction from the Council. Shockingly, Luke captures the Sanhedrin's response in a single verse:

> *Now when they saw the boldness of Peter and John, and perceived that they were uneducated, common men, they were astonished. And they recognized that they had been with Jesus.*
>
> Acts 4:13

Peter and John rocked these leaders more by who they were than by what they said. The two men were simply being themselves, filled with the Holy Spirit (Acts 4:8). The only explanation the Council had for the kind of men standing before them was that they had been with Jesus. But there's more—when believers in Jerusalem heard about the interrogation, they also prayed for boldness to preach the Word of God, and God answered them (Acts 4:31).

The way God partners with us to advance the kingdom may look different than Peter's calling or John's, yet we are similar men. As we live with Jesus in more areas of our hearts and lives, we also become more fully the unique men of gravity that God created us to be.

Life with Jesus is not a means to an end, of course. But I don't think we should worry about our motives for spending time with Him. If we begin opening hidden rooms to Jesus solely to find relief and progress, superb. This growth process has a built-in mechanism to protect us from seeing the Lord in the months and years ahead only as a way forward. The more courageous and honest we are with Him, the more we realize His presence means more to us than whatever we ask of Him. He alone becomes our portion and our cup (Ps. 16:5). Men and women around us will sense this, and they will draw closer to Him.

Amen.

Well, brother, it is hard to say goodbye. It's been my great privilege to walk with you these last few months. Bless you now as we part ways and travel on with God. With respect and affection, I say farewell and ask you to pray for me as I pray for you.

Prayer Project

1. Ask the Lord, "God, do I have a gut-level sense of the distinction between being more capable and being different? How would I describe this distinction? Do I believe that the world needs more of one than the other? Why?"

2. Ask the Lord, "Lord, what has happened in the time we've spent together in this guidebook? What have you been up to? What has the experience been like for me?"

3. Ask the Lord, "How do I feel about this book coming to a close? Where does it leave me?"

4. Ask the Lord, "Where do we go from here, God? What are your desires? What are my intentions?"

5. Spend some time resting with God and enjoying His presence.

Appendix 1

Some Thoughts on Lust

So many of us struggle with this part of our character. Actually, the vast majority of men do. I fought a long battle with lust as well, and I want to share some of the most helpful things I learned. First, we will take a fresh look at what is perhaps the highest personal cost of sexual sin. Second, we'll outline a multidimensional and balanced approach to lust that we can use to combat this powerful and insidious adversary.

The high price we pay for sexual sin

We must speak directly now and face a terrible fact: If we give ourselves over to sexual sin, we will likely experience only limited development in other parts of our character. I realize this is a dramatic statement, brother. And there are exceptions, of course. However, the rule of thumb holds true for most of us. Here's why: sexual sin obliterates our perspective.

When we allow lust to take up residence in our souls, we numb ourselves to God's presence and activity in our lives. We don't see clearly—other parts of our character that demand attention may go unnoticed. Or, if we do notice these troubled areas of our hearts, we often don't recognize their seriousness or make meaningful headway toward change. In a real sense, a pervasive fog of spiritual numbness holds us in darkness and threatens to snuff out the light of reality.

We believe lies when living in this state. Alarming statistics on Christian men engaged with pornography, for example, may register temporary pangs of guilt and shame but do not compel us to act. Researchers concluded in 2022 that nearly 70 percent of church-going men view porn regularly.[18] However, statistics like this one don't startle us anymore. Instead, we find them strangely comforting. We're in good company, right? If 70 percent of all Christian men regularly engage in sexual sin, then we must be doing reasonably well. We're simply robust men sentenced to live with an understandable shortcoming.

Of course, this is a lie.

Let's recover a solid perspective through two steps. One, accept the fact that we believe a lie from the enemy when we resign our souls to lust. Sexual sin is not an unconquerable foe. God did not acquiesce here. He did not agree that sensuality is an irresistible force that will routinely overpower us despite our best and reasonable efforts to stand firm. Second, we need to initiate friendships with the 30 percent of men who walk in sexual wholeness. When I made friends with "thirty-percenters" who chose not to view porn, my life began to change. I started to pile up more wins in my fight against lust.

An approach to combating lust—Act aggressively

Two friends in particular taught me a three-pronged approach to my long-standing problem: flee, learn, and fight. I started with "flee" and still employ this strategy today.

Flee

A couple of Scripture passages, in addition to my own life lessons, helped me understand the powerful deception of lust, as well as the importance of running:

> *Flee from sexual immorality.*   1 Corinthians 6:18

> *You have heard that it was said, "You shall not commit adultery." But I say to you that <u>everyone who looks at a woman with lustful intent has already committed adultery with her in his heart.</u>*
> Matthew 5:27-28, emphasis mine

---

18 Landon Tucker, "Hope in the Midst of Porn Addiction," Lifeway Voices, Lifeway Christian Resources, January 20, 2022, https://voices.lifeway.com/culture-current-events/hope-in-the-midst-of-porn-addiction/.

These verses and others like them began to sober me up.

One of my friends had found a practical way to flee, and I adopted it: bounce and focus. Here's what this approach looks like. When our eyes fall upon a woman wearing clothes that celebrate her features, for example, we quickly bounce our eyes off her and focus hard on something else. No lingering. No second looks. If our eyes find a tree immediately after bouncing, we might focus on the leaves—their color, shape, stems, and number. If we land on a car, maybe we study the design of its wheels or wonder about its aerodynamics. The idea is to shut down our mind's pursuit of the sensual image that caught our eye.

It works. And like other behaviors, it is habit-forming. If we employ the method for a solid couple of months, our eyes automatically bounce and focus. It cuts off a vast number of new mental pictures that would inflame our sexual urges. Of course, our battle is not only with new material. Most of us have lots of images already stored in our brains. How do we flee from them?

Fortunately, our new habit helps us in these moments, too. If we quickly shift our minds to some other topic or activity and focus hard on it, we will not feast on the tantalizing thoughts and images that float up from mental storage. I found that I often had to add physical movement to this mental strategy as well. If sitting down when tempted, I got up and went to another part of the house or office. A change of environment often puts distance between us and those alluring visions.

Of course, it isn't easy to intentionally form a habit that prevents us from doing something we desperately want. But it can be done. Many men develop this habit. It slows down our "lust life" enough to bring a better perspective on our condition and a deeper desire for healthier living.

Learn

Search me, O God, and know my heart! Try me and know my thoughts! And see if there be any grievous way in me, and lead me in the way everlasting!

Psalm 139:23-24

There is much to learn once we are in the room with Jesus. Some topics are tactical in nature. For example, if we slip into fantasy, pornography, or acting out, we can ask the Lord, "What happened there? What was the trigger? How did I get moving in that direction? What warnings did I override, and how did I quash them?" We can begin to ask more general tactical questions as well: "When am I most vulnerable to sexual temptation? In what locations do I find myself most tempted? What concrete changes would be helpful? What resources are available to me?" In conversations like these, we learn a lot about taking better care of ourselves so we don't get overtired, frustrated, stressed out, or super-bored. We recognize places and activities that overstimulate us and choose to avoid them. For example, we might need to stay clear of the beach or pool when many sunbathers pour in. Maybe we decide to screen movies and television shows differently or throw away parts of the Sunday paper.

At some point, we'll want to shift from tactical questions to strategic queries. We need to move beyond triggers and talk about susceptibility. For example, we might ask Jesus, "What makes me so vulnerable to sexual temptation? What areas of my life or pockets of my heart do I want to run from and numb? Why? How do I deal with these troubled parts of my character differently? What does healthy sexuality look like for men anyway?"

As time and conversations in the room passed, I noticed two inclinations growing inside me. One was that I seemed to be less tightly wound about my preferred method of fleeing sexual images and thoughts. Bouncing my eyes and focusing my mind became more habitual and comfortable now. I also noticed that when sensual content did make its way into my mind, and I acknowledged it, I could sometimes let it dissipate and pass without chasing after it. I could move on without having to refocus hard or physically move. This additional way of dealing with temptation complimented my core strategy for flight very well.

The second inclination that developed in the room with Jesus rocked me with force and trepidation. I found myself standing at a new threshold and knew I had to cross over to a place where things would never be the same. It was time to fight!

Fight

Submit yourselves therefore to God. Resist the devil, and he will flee from you.

James 4:7

We might lack the strength of resolve to stand up to the enemy until we know what we want and trust Jesus to provide the power we need to go after it. I knew I wasn't ready to fight when Jesus and I first entered my room called "Lust." Flight served me well for quite a while, and I have not outgrown it. I still fly fast when necessary. But "fight" had to enter the picture if I wanted to break through enemy defenses and occupy the land of my inheritance—a spacious land of freedom and light. I was reluctant to take this step when the inclination first emerged. But something else had formed inside me, too: a disposition that thrust me forward when Jesus pushed. This new mentality came with the voice of authority: "Enough!"

Almost unawares, part of our soul grows over time to despise the power lust has over us. We detest the cold fact that this sin dominated and mastered us. We loathe feeling compromised, soiled, and powerless. Raw hate now fuels our courage. Our backs stiffen up. Our foreheads harden. We find ourselves refusing to walk around with part of our hearts more devoted to sin than to God. "This will not stand!" we think. So, finally, we stand with Jesus and tell enemy forces face-to-face—in the name of Jesus Christ and in His strength alone—that they are living on the ground that is rightfully ours and that we will occupy immediately. They must step off as we step on. From that moment forward, we intend to live an obedient life in the power of the Spirit in this part of our character.

Jesus and I crossed over many years ago, but the story didn't end there. The enemy and my flesh did not abandon all efforts to harass me. Temptations did not cease—the requirement for ongoing watchfulness stands firmly in place today. I also learned that when we stop doing something we shouldn't do, we know more about why we did it. Areas of challenge and discontent in my life came to the fore now; some needed my attention and care. But above all, I slowly began to feel right-sized. I was bigger than I used to be. And I carried within me a much greater capacity to grow and to become the man I was meant to be.

However, I don't think we need to convince ourselves of the many life-giving benefits of obedience. It is enough that God commands it, and we can trust His unwavering desire for our good in all things. He does not deprive us of something here. He gives us something.

We cannot go wrong with nearness and love to move toward His gift. A more profound connection with Jesus in this room and with other men who are further along and wiser than we are will launch us on our adventure toward more life. So, I leave you in good hands. Peace, brother. All will be well.

Appendix 2

Spiritual Direction

To learn more about the ministry of spiritual direction, I recommend the Evangelical Spiritual Directors Association (ESDA). I'm a member of ESDA, part of Grafted Life Ministries. Go to graftedlife.org and click "Spiritual Direction" to read a short description of direction and learn how to locate a spiritual director who might be a good fit for you.

www.ingramcontent.com/pod-product-compliance
Lightning Source LLC
Chambersburg PA
CBHW020422130626
46549CB00006B/2699